AF429699

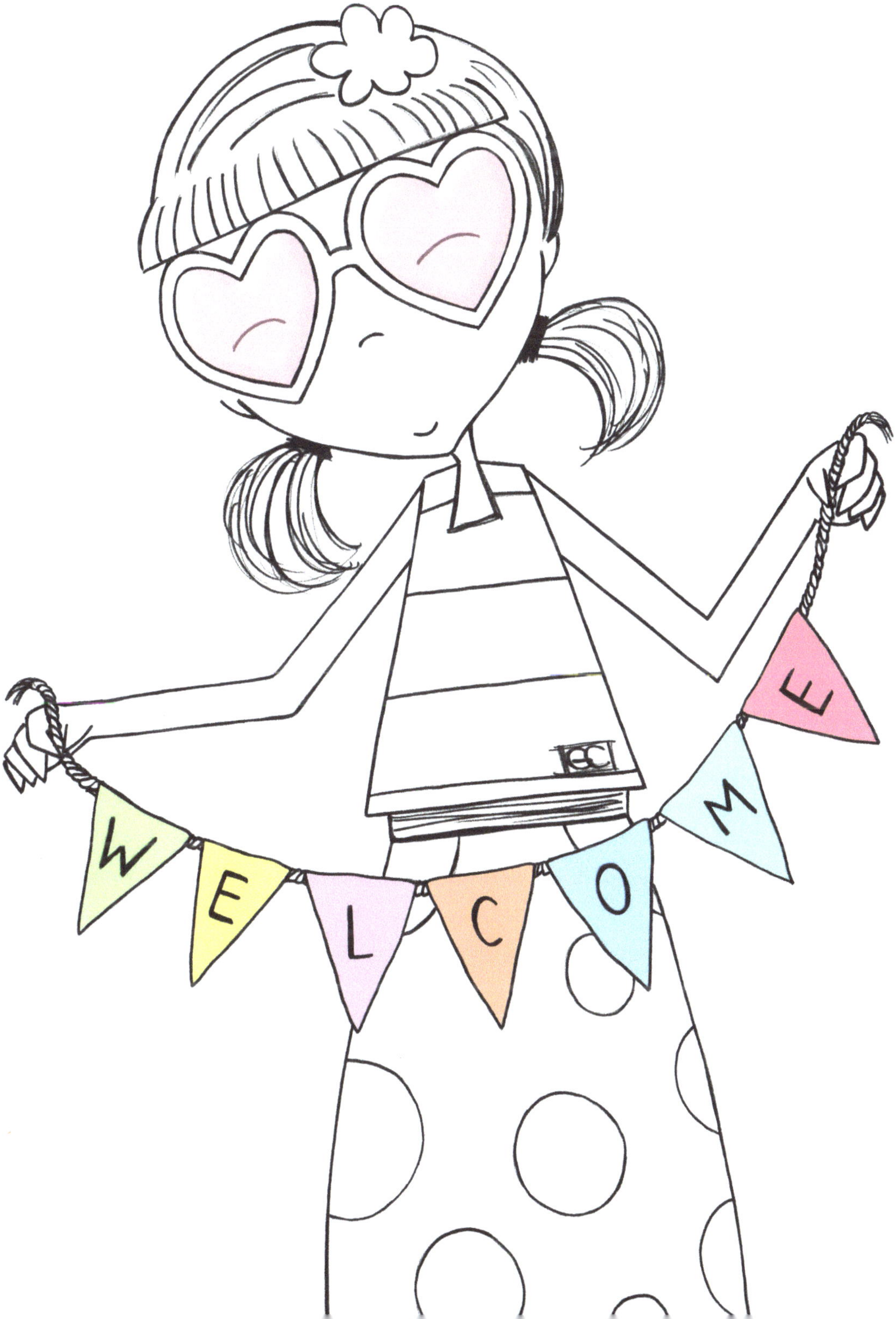

WELCOME

THREE THINGS TO KNOW
BEFORE DIVING INTO YOUR BOOK:

1. There's **no right or wrong order** to approach this volume:
jump about from page to page, choosing the one that inspires you in that moment!

2. Sketching and drawing are certainly not the only ways you can follow the book prompts!
In fact, I invite you to **shape the activities** according to the materials and techniques you prefer!
You might take pictures, using the book as a scrapbook album,
decide to make collages with paper scraps or clippings,
choose to write down thoughts, turning these pages into a unique journal...
Feel free to experiment without pressure or judgment!

3. **Grown-ups and Kids 7+** will make full use of this book,
but many pages are suitable for 5 and 6 year olds as well, with a bit of help from an adult.

... AND ONE TIP: add a signature and date to your sheets!
It would be super fun to re-work on the same prompt
at different times, comparing all the versions!

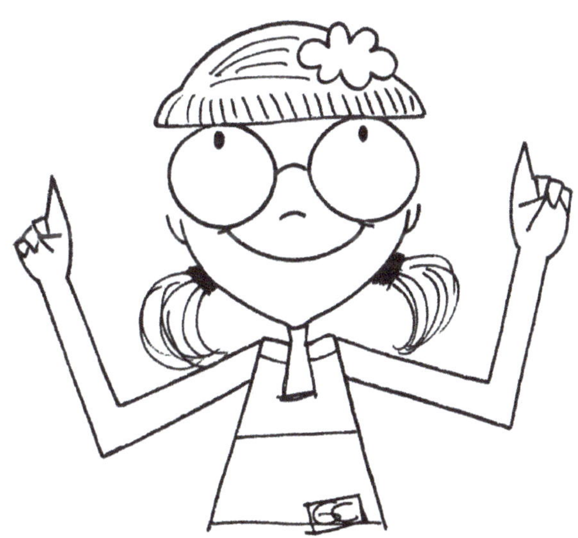

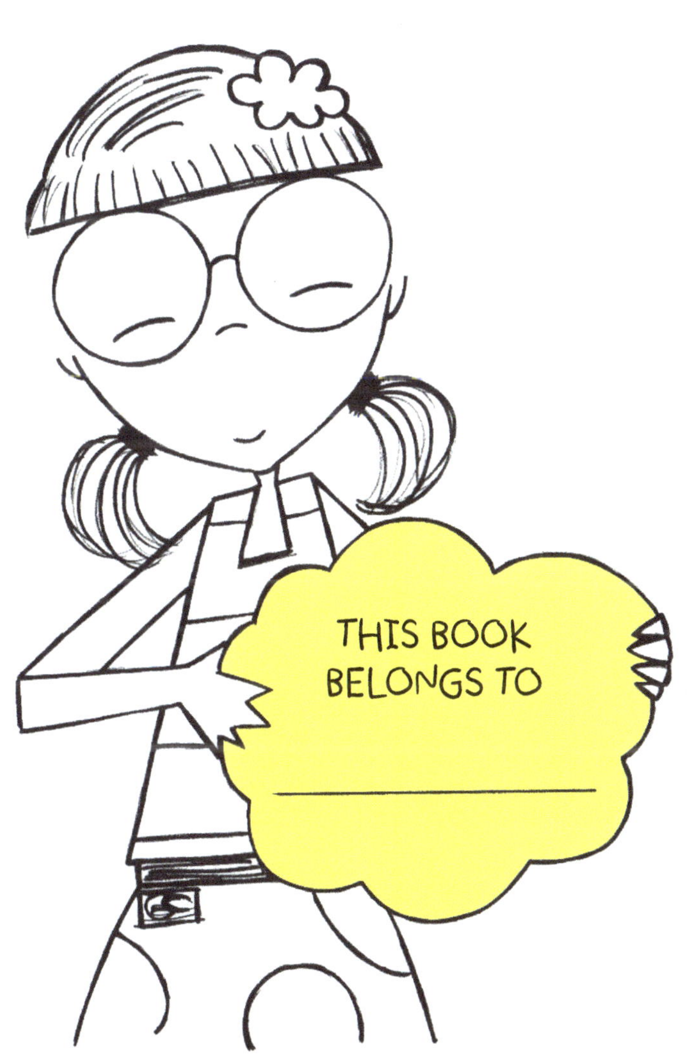
THIS BOOK
BELONGS TO
____

- ☐ ADVENTURES
- ☐ SEASONS
- ☐ SCIENCE
- ☐ RELAX
- ☐ OBSERVATION
- ☐ NATURE
- ☐ MOMENTS
- ☐ TRANSPORTATION
- ☐ STYLE
- ☐ MUSIC
- ☐ KINDNESS
- ☐ IMAGINATION
- ☐ EXPERIENCES
- ☐ SURPRISES
- ☐ PLACES
- ☐ HABITS
- ☐ FRIENDSHIP
- ☐ LEARNING
- ☐ CRAFT
- ☐ BEAUTY
- ☐ PATIENCE
- ☐ WORDS
- ☐ TRAVELS
- ☐ TRANSFORMATION
- ☐ BALANCE

- ☐ TECHNOLOGY
- ☐ STORIES
- ☐ GRATITUDE
- ☐ FUN
- ☐ FANTASY
- ☐ FOOD
- ☐ FAMILY
- ☐ GENEROSITY
- ☐ EXPLORATION
- ☐ ENERGY
- ☐ CURIOSITY
- ☐ DREAMS
- ☐ CELEBRATION
- ☐ ART
- ☐ BOOKS
- ☐ CREATIVITY
- ☐ LOVE
- ☐ GAMES
- ☐ FUTURE WORLD
- ☐ SPACES
- ☐ COLORS
- ☐ ANIMALS
- ☐ HOLIDAYS
- ☐ HAPPINESS
- ☐ REMINDERS

ADVENTURES

LOOK AT WHAT FLORA HAS JUST FOUND! WHAT WILL THIS KEY OPEN???

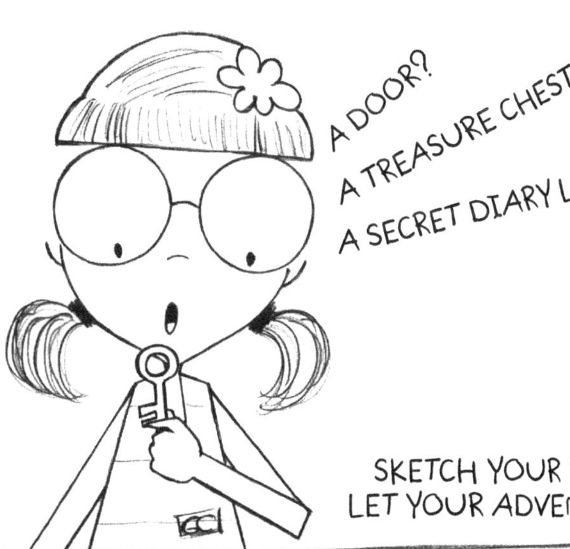

SKETCH YOUR IDEAS AND
LET YOUR ADVENTURE BEGIN!

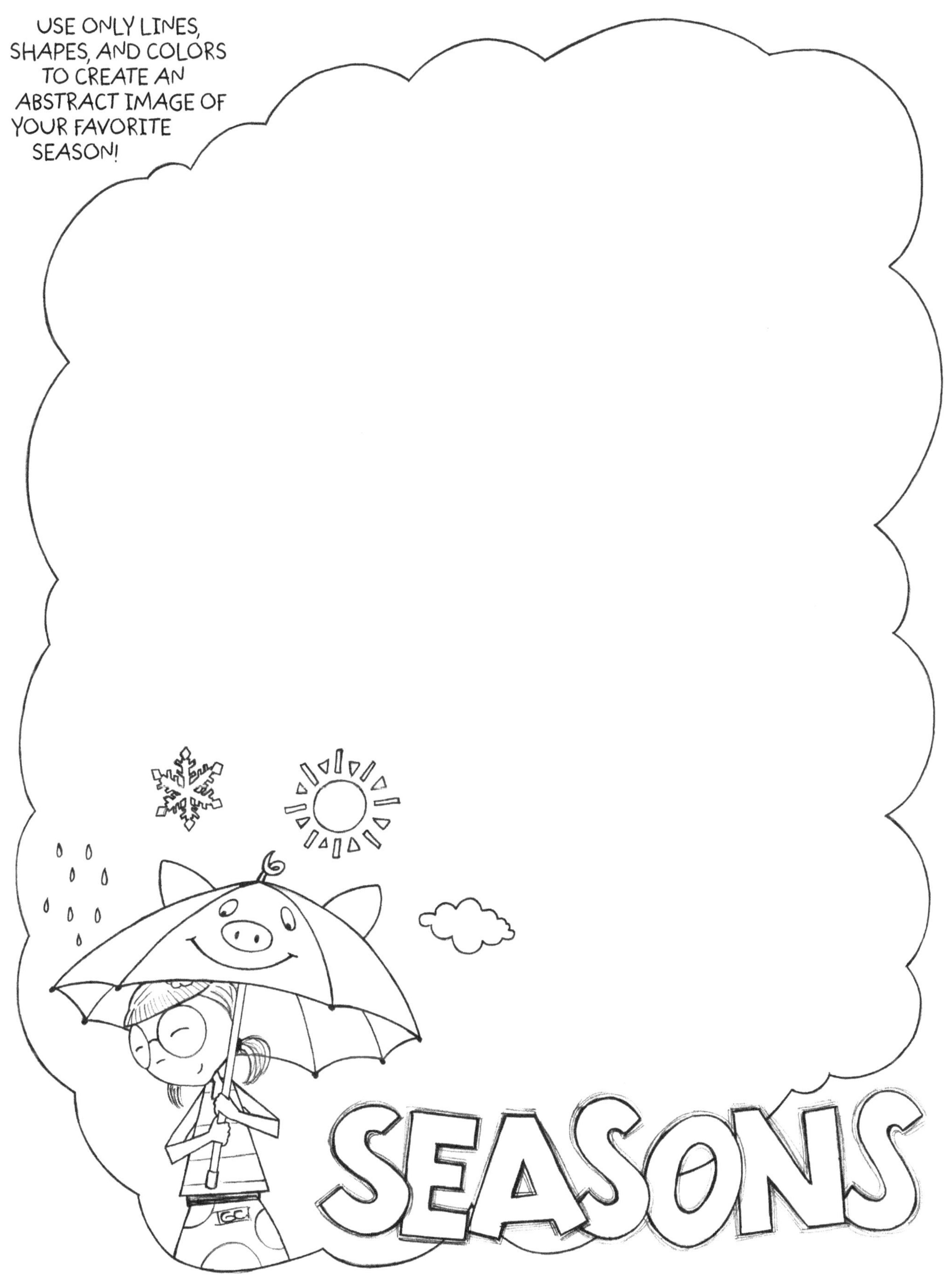
USE ONLY LINES, SHAPES, AND COLORS TO CREATE AN ABSTRACT IMAGE OF YOUR FAVORITE SEASON!
SEASONS

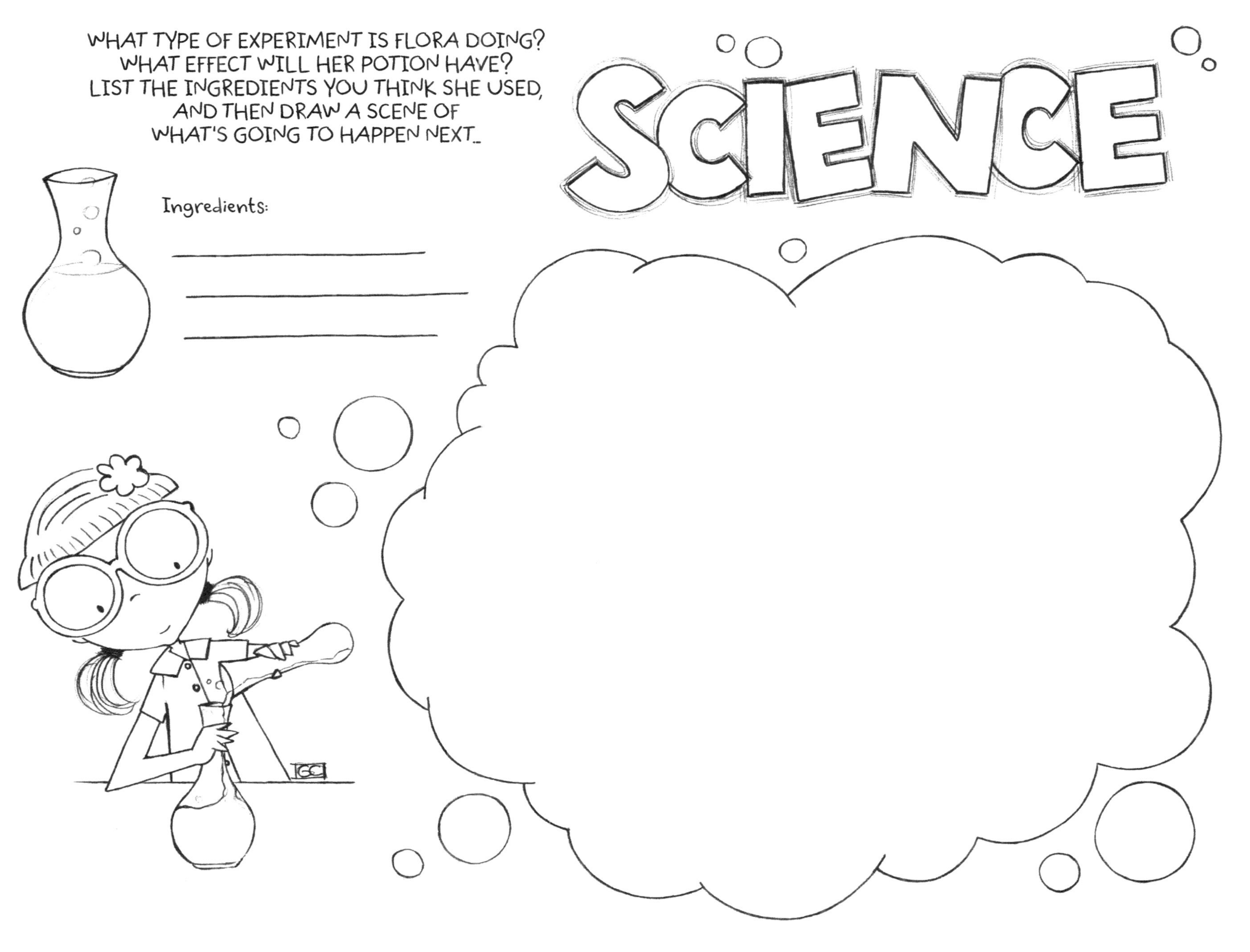

SCIENCE
WHAT TYPE OF EXPERIMENT IS FLORA DOING?
WHAT EFFECT WILL HER POTION HAVE?
LIST THE INGREDIENTS YOU THINK SHE USED,
AND THEN DRAW A SCENE OF
WHAT'S GOING TO HAPPEN NEXT...
Ingredients:

RELAX

WHERE IS THE PLACE YOU GO
TO RELAX? WHAT'S THE
SPECIAL SPACE THAT MAKES
YOU FEEL COMFORTABLE,
SAFE, AND CALM?

FLORA FOUND THE
PERFECT SPOT IN HER TENT.
HOW ABOUT YOU?

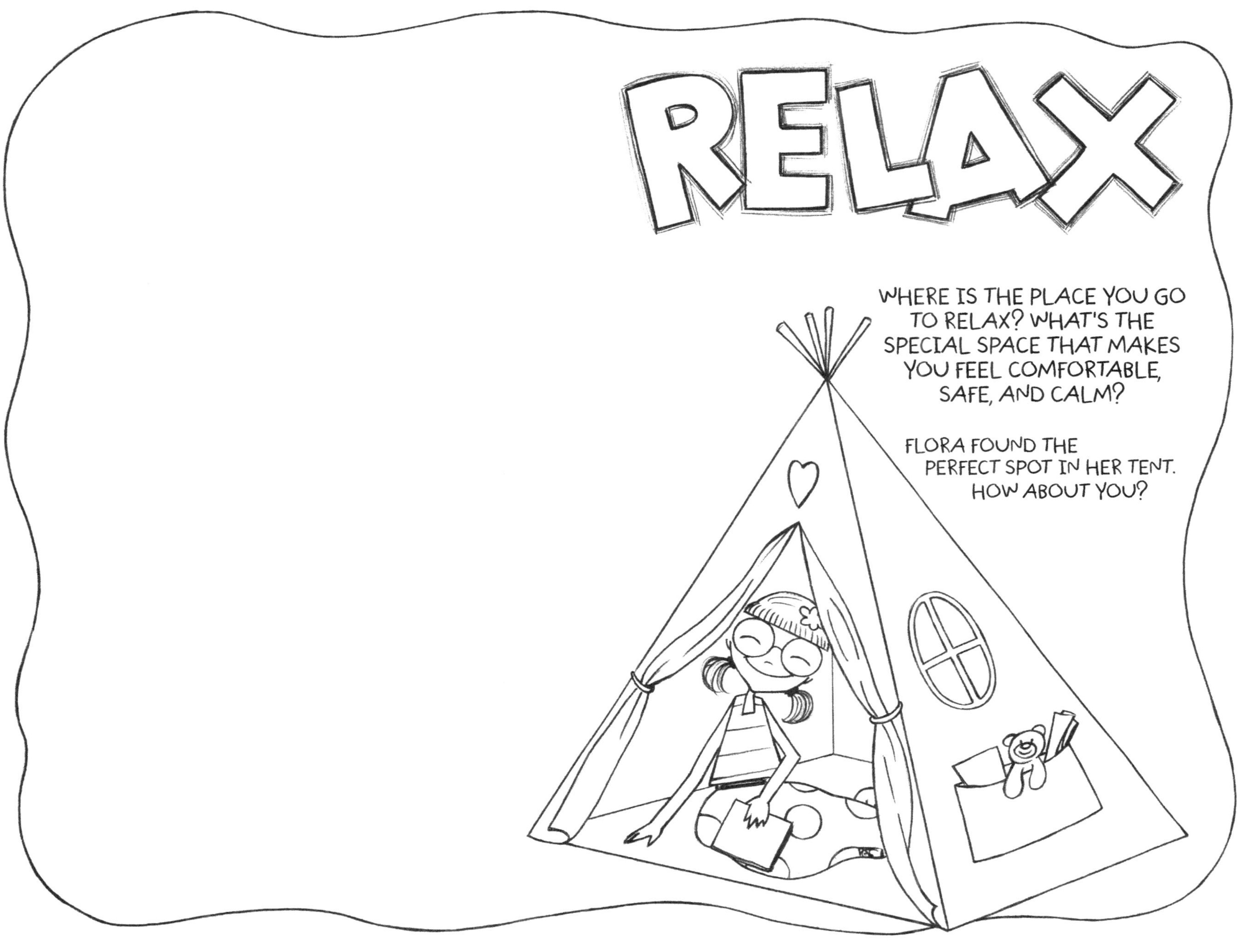

OBSERVATION

FLORA LOVES TO OBSERVE CLOSELY THE LITTLE DETAILS AROUND HER!
THERE'S SO MUCH TO BE CURIOUS ABOUT!
IN THE PLACE YOU ARE RIGHT NOW, SPOT SOME OBJECTS
THAT CAPTURE YOUR ATTENTION, AND DRAW WHAT YOU SEE!

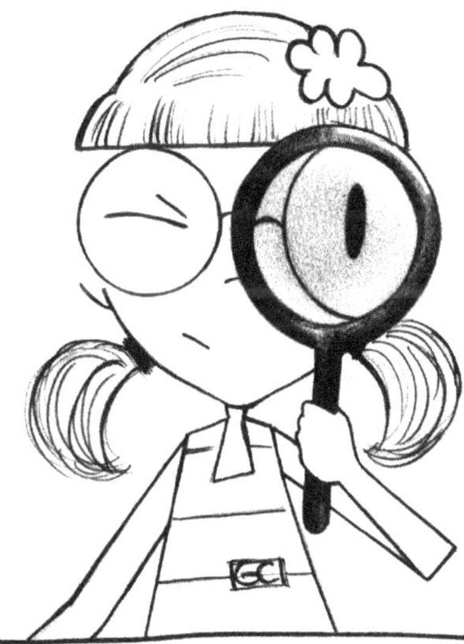

NATURE

HOW DO YOU IMAGINE FLORA'S GARDEN?
WHAT COLORS, FLAVORS, SMELLS?
ARE THERE ANY ANIMALS?
COMPLETE THE SCENE BY DRAWING
FLOWERS, PLANTS,
NATURAL ELEMENTS...

MOMENTS

WHAT WAS A MEMORABLE DAY IN YOUR LIFE? AN UNFORGETTABLE MOMENT YOU SPENT WITH YOUR FAMILY OR FRIENDS? WHAT'S A SPECIAL EXPERIENCE OR A MEANINGFUL EVENT THAT YOU'LL REMEMBER FOREVER? SKETCH A SCENE!

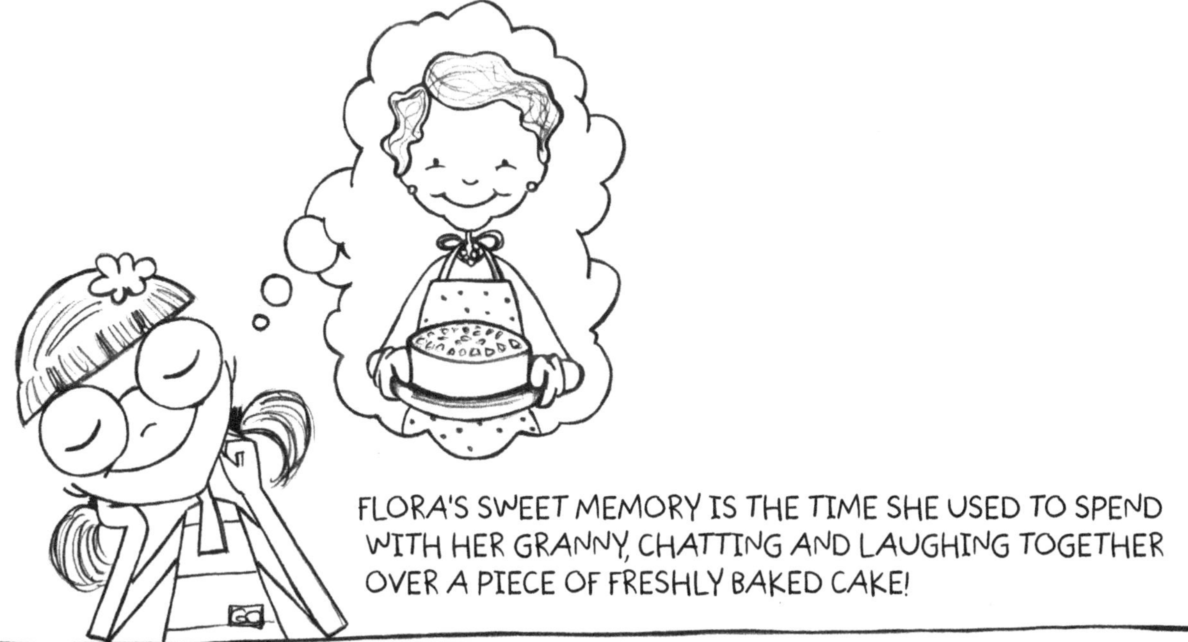

FLORA'S SWEET MEMORY IS THE TIME SHE USED TO SPEND WITH HER GRANNY, CHATTING AND LAUGHING TOGETHER OVER A PIECE OF FRESHLY BAKED CAKE!

TRANSPORTATION

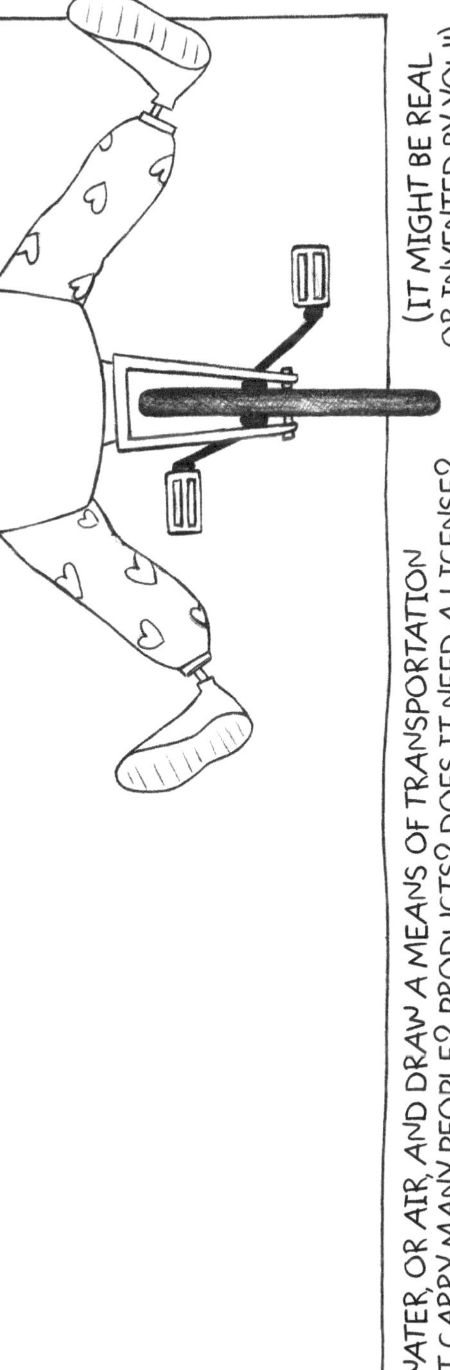

CHOOSE LAND, WATER, OR AIR, AND DRAW A MEANS OF TRANSPORTATION RELATED TO IT! DOES IT CARRY MANY PEOPLE? PRODUCTS? DOES IT NEED A LICENSE? (IT MIGHT BE REAL OR INVENTED BY YOU!)

WHAT ARE YOUR FAVORITE PIECES
OF CLOTHING IN YOUR CLOSET?
WHY DO YOU LIKE THEM?
SKETCH THE ITEM OR OUTFIT
THAT BEST REPRESENTS YOU!

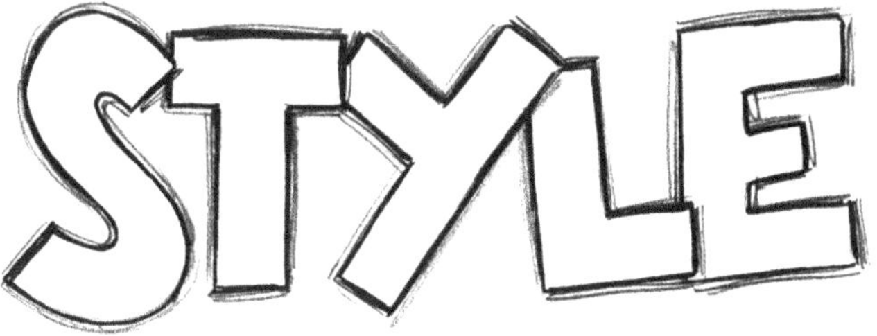

STYLE

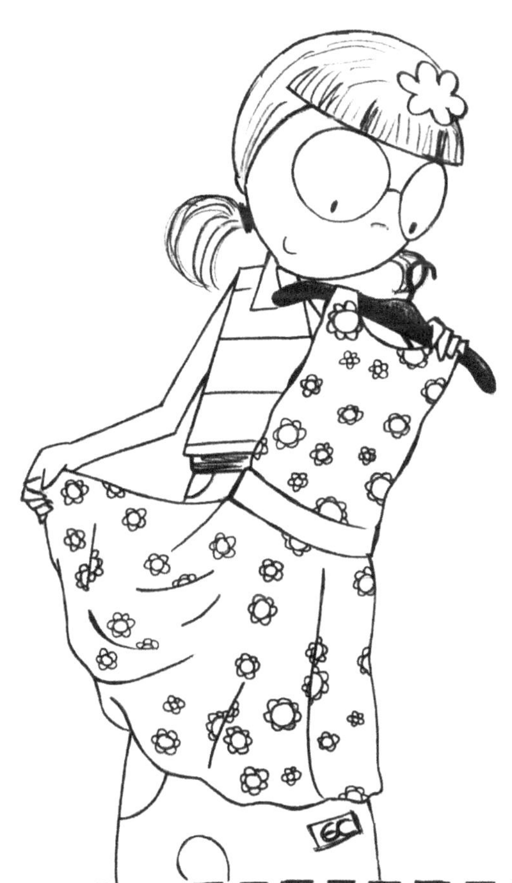

ILLUSTRATE A SONG!
LISTEN TO A PIECE OF MUSIC
AND LET THE LYRICS, THE RHYTHM,
AND THE MOOD INSPIRE YOU!
HOW DOES THIS SONG
MAKE YOU FEEL?

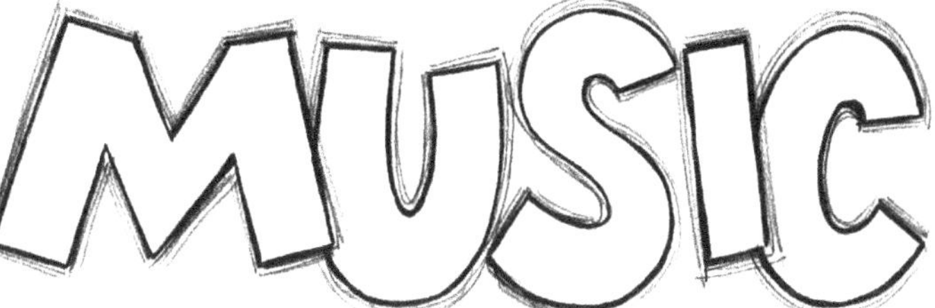
MUSIC

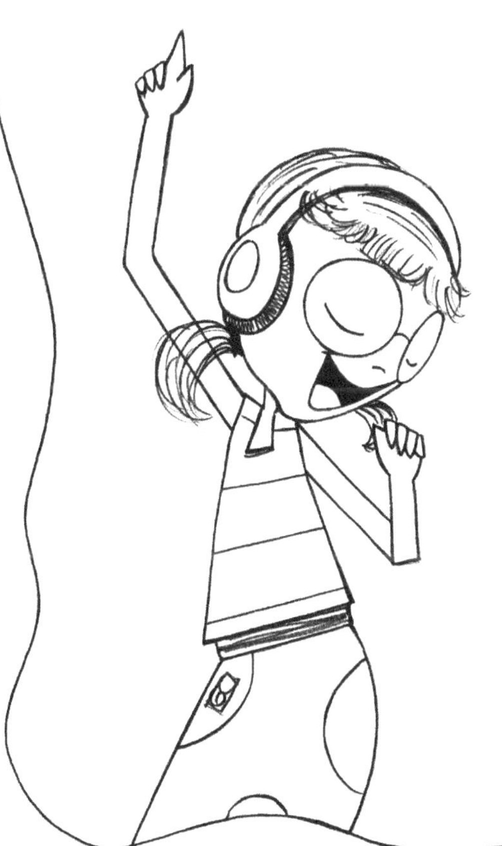

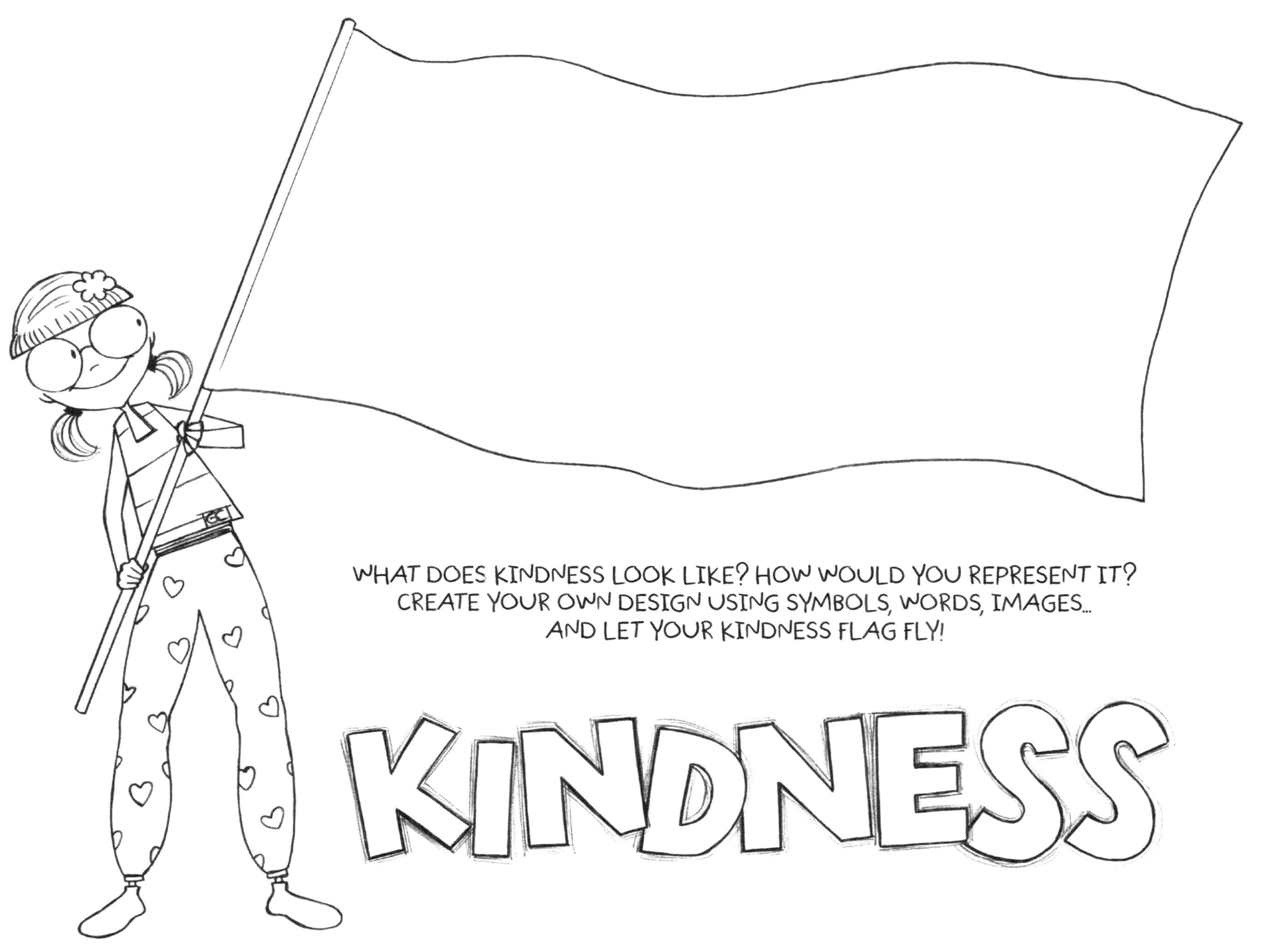

WHAT DOES KINDNESS LOOK LIKE? HOW WOULD YOU REPRESENT IT?
CREATE YOUR OWN DESIGN USING SYMBOLS, WORDS, IMAGES...
AND LET YOUR KINDNESS FLAG FLY!
KINDNESS

IMAGINATION

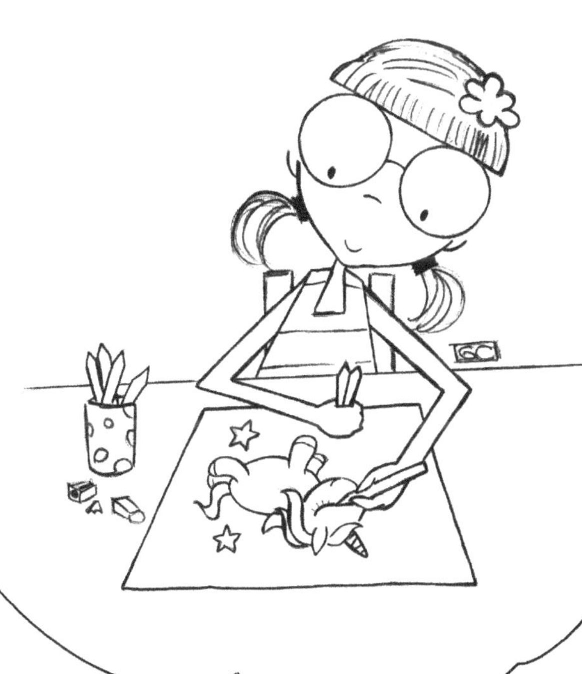

EXPERIENCES

SOMETHING YOU CAN HEAR

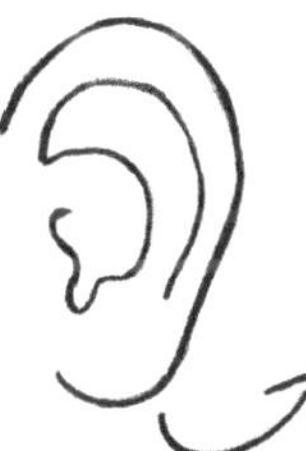

SOMETHING YOU CAN SMELL

SOMETHING YOU CAN TASTE

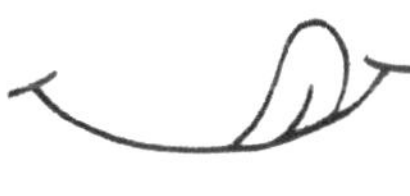

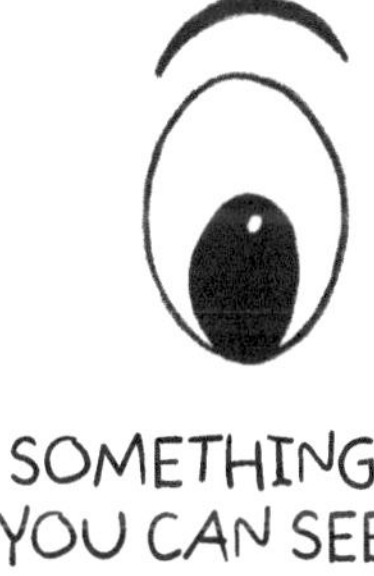

SOMETHING YOU CAN SEE

SOMETHING YOU CAN TOUCH

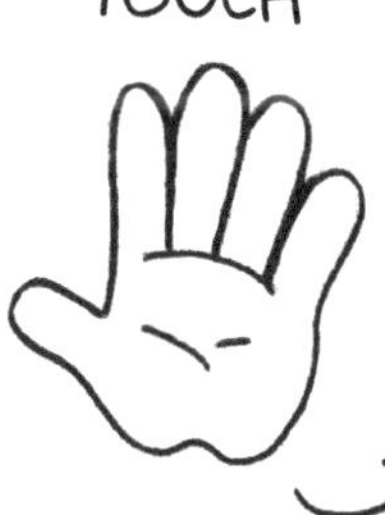

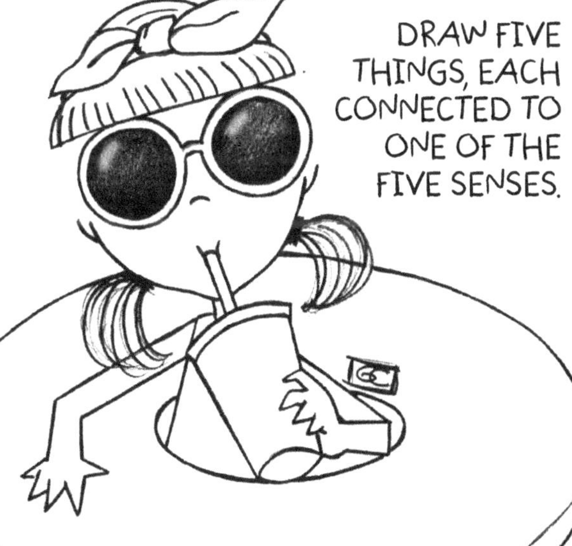

DRAW FIVE THINGS, EACH CONNECTED TO ONE OF THE FIVE SENSES.

SURPRISES

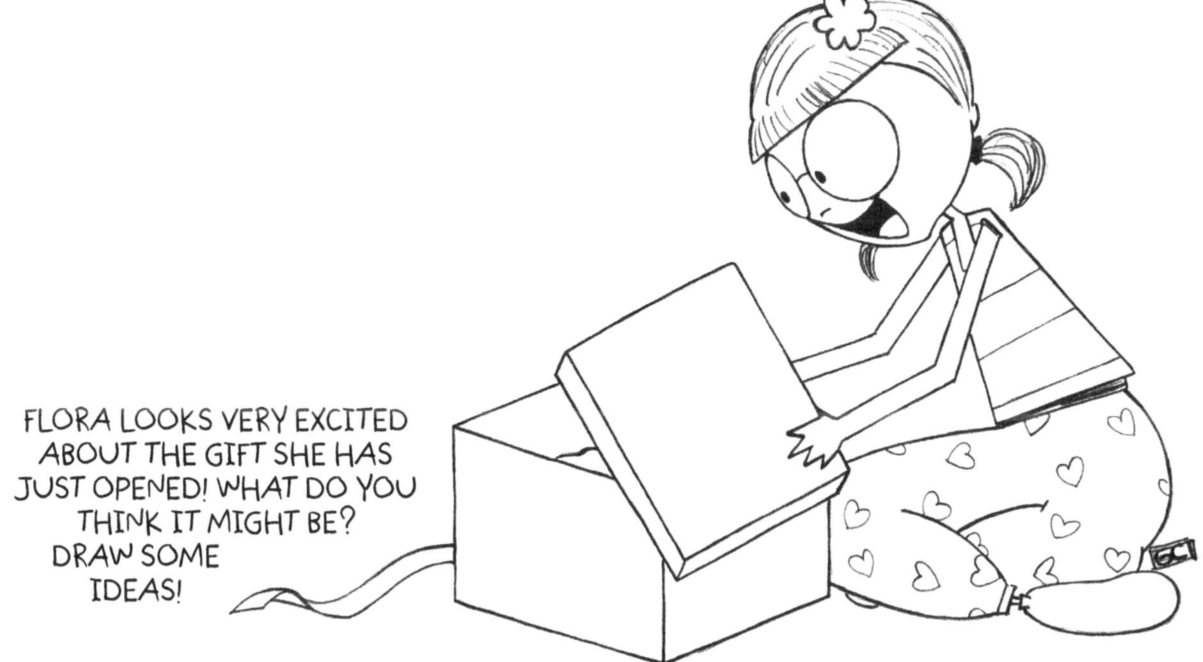

FLORA LOOKS VERY EXCITED
ABOUT THE GIFT SHE HAS
JUST OPENED! WHAT DO YOU
THINK IT MIGHT BE?
DRAW SOME
IDEAS!

PLACES

CREATE YOUR OWN COUNTRY!

NAME: _______________________

OUTLINE
THE SHAPE
OF YOUR
COUNTRY

WHAT'S THE MOST POPULAR FOOD?

DESIGN THE NATIONAL FLAG
(ARE THERE ANY COLORS OR SYMBOLS
THAT BEST REPRESENT YOUR COUNTRY?)

DESIGN ONE TRADITIONAL
ITEM OF CLOTHING

DRAW A PICTURE OF
A FAMOUS TOURIST ATTRACTION
(A BUILDING, A PARK, A MONUMENT...)

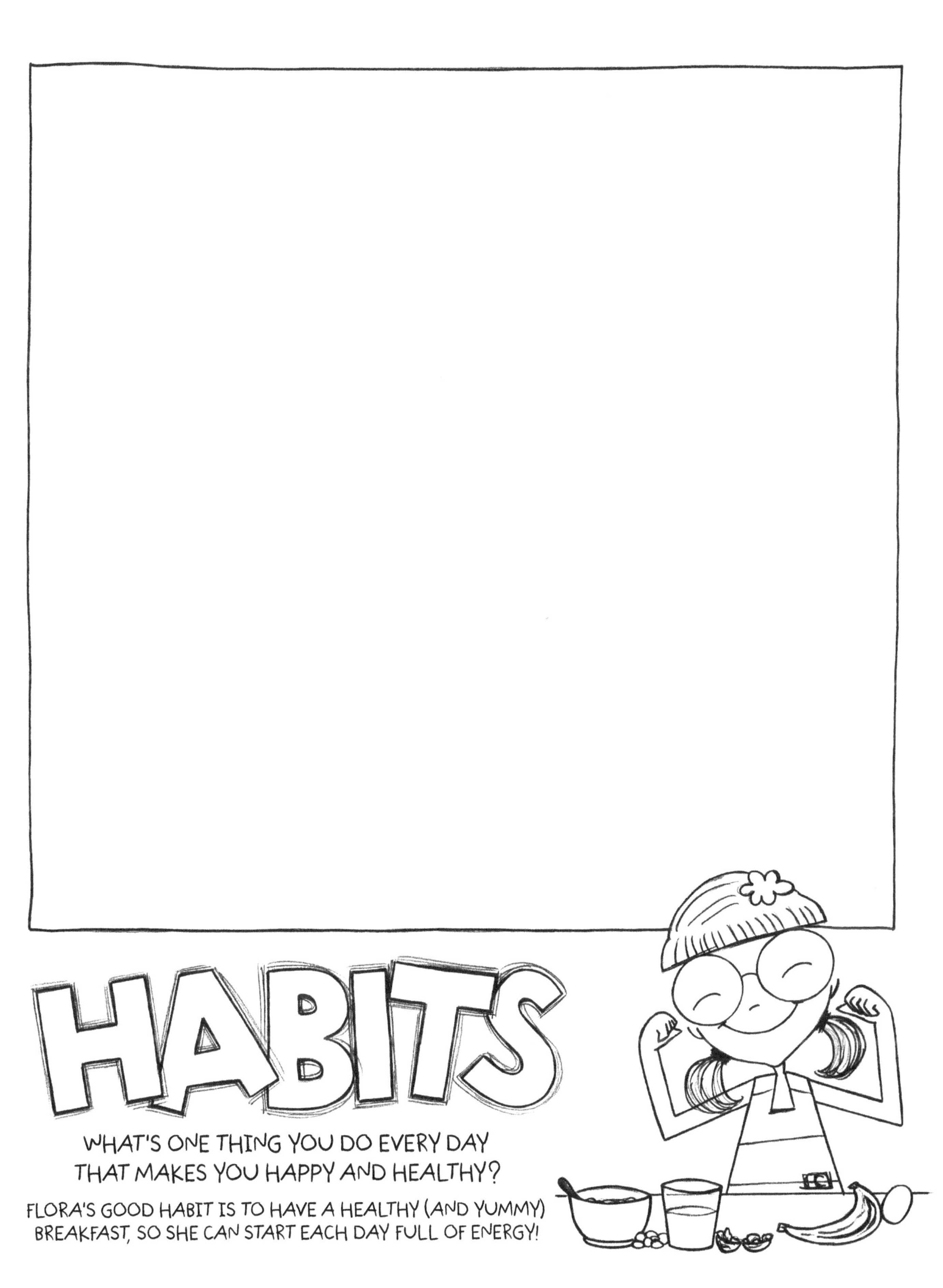

HABITS
WHAT'S ONE THING YOU DO EVERY DAY
THAT MAKES YOU HAPPY AND HEALTHY?
FLORA'S GOOD HABIT IS TO HAVE A HEALTHY (AND YUMMY)
BREAKFAST, SO SHE CAN START EACH DAY FULL OF ENERGY!

FRIENDSHIPS ARE VERY IMPORTANT IN FLORA'S LIFE!
SHE WOULD LOVE TO HAVE A NEW FRIEND CREATED BY YOU!
DRAW A PERSON, AN ANIMAL, AN IMAGINARY CHARACTER...
GIVE THEM A NAME, AND THINK ABOUT THEIR QUALITIES.
WHAT MAKES A GOOD FRIEND?
FLORA CAN'T WAIT TO MEET
HER NEW ADVENTURE COMPANION!

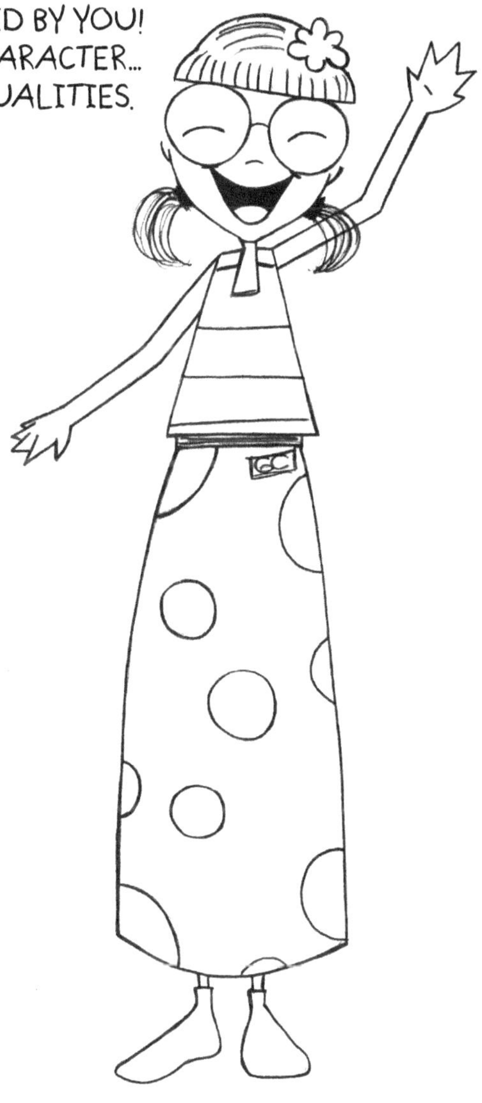

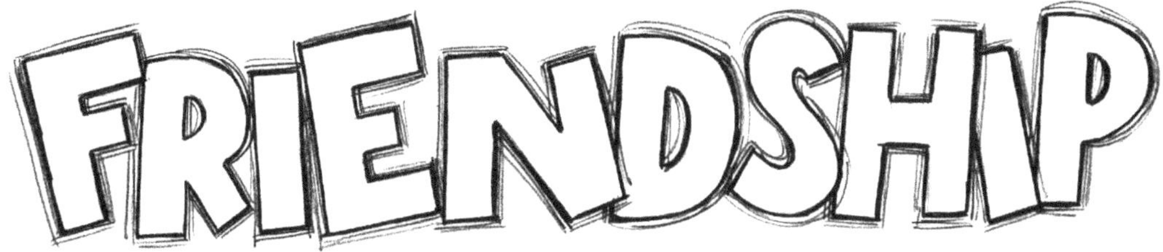

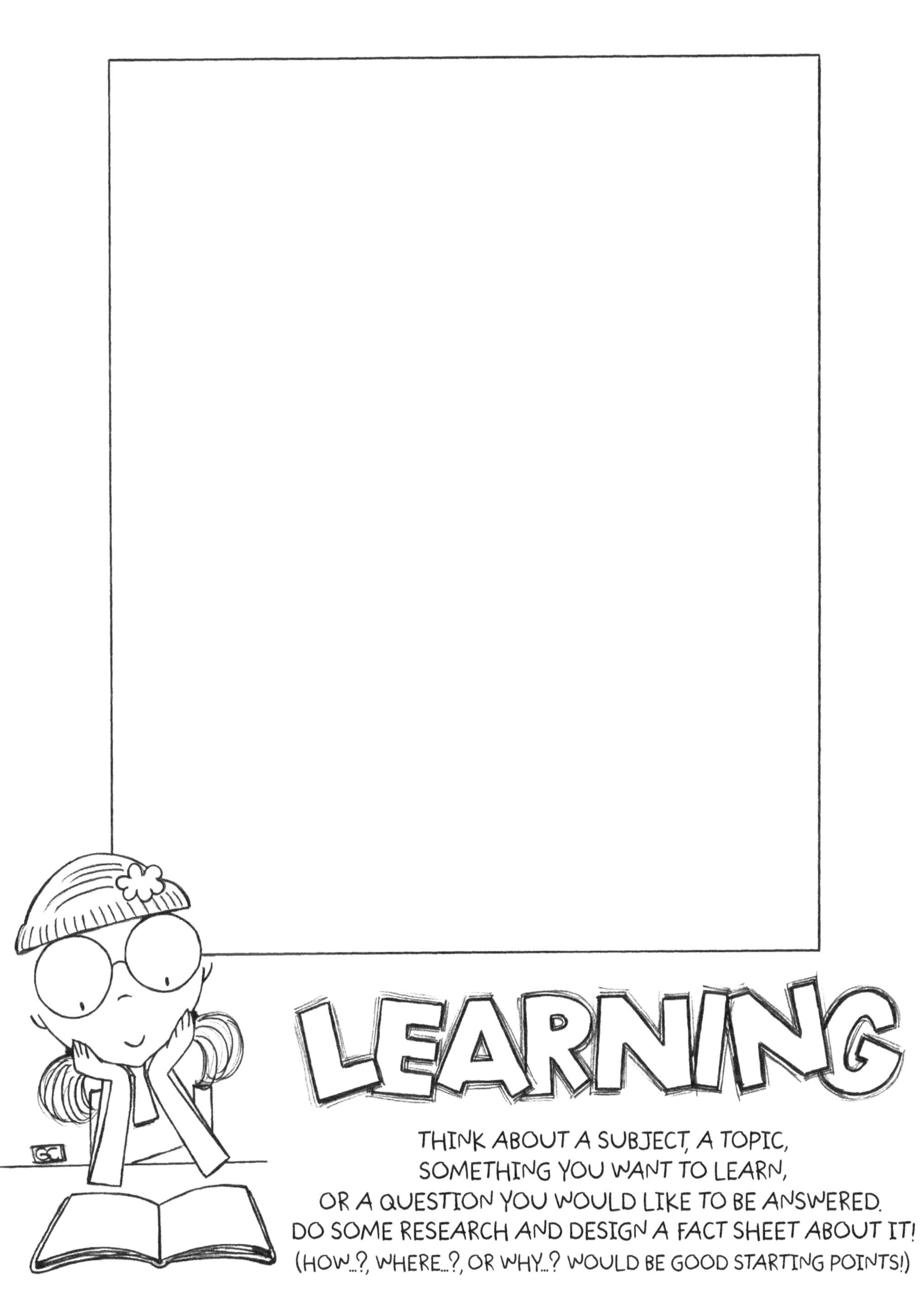

LEARNING
THINK ABOUT A SUBJECT, A TOPIC,
SOMETHING YOU WANT TO LEARN,
OR A QUESTION YOU WOULD LIKE TO BE ANSWERED.
DO SOME RESEARCH AND DESIGN A FACT SHEET ABOUT IT!
(HOW...?, WHERE...?, OR WHY...? WOULD BE GOOD STARTING POINTS!)

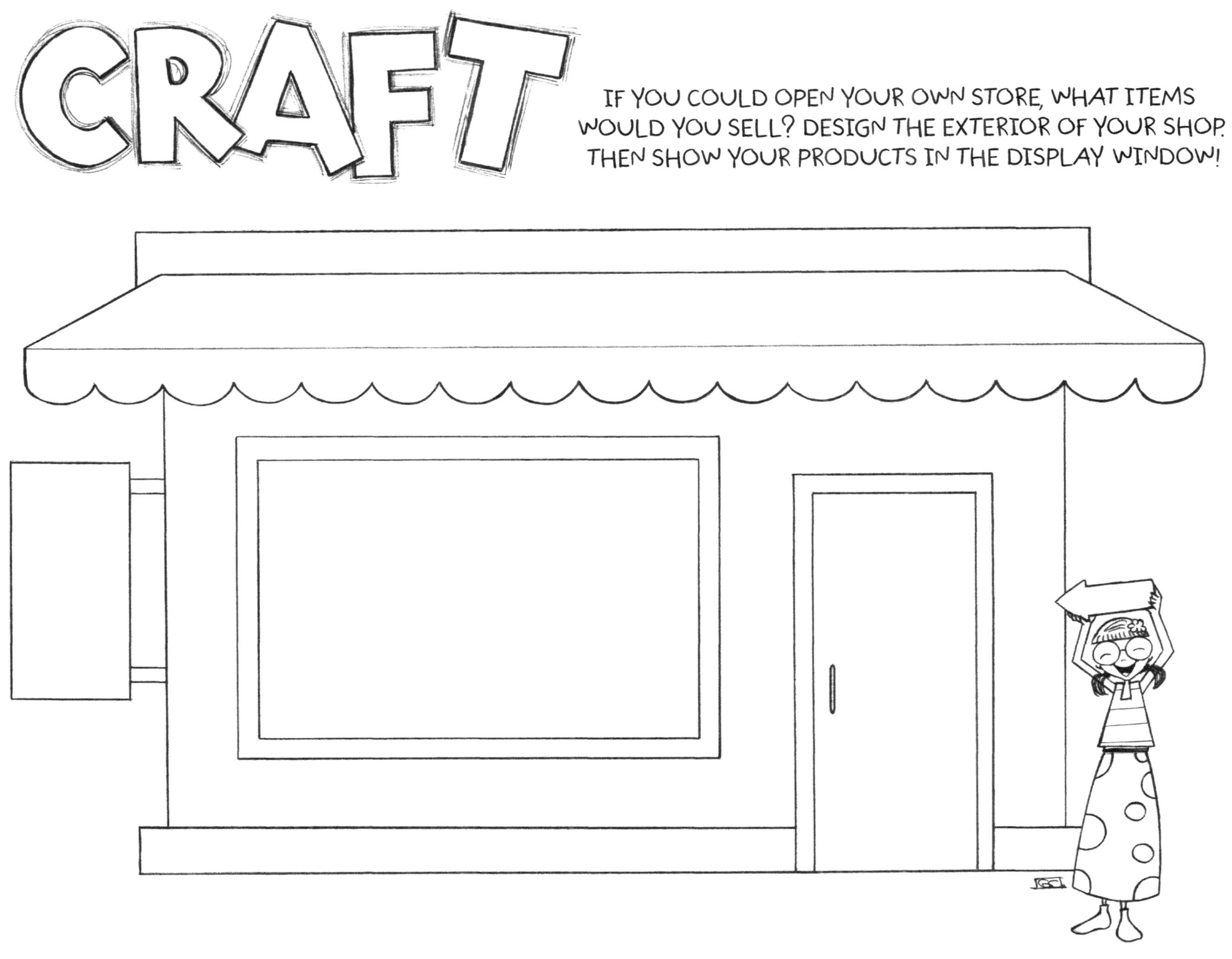

CRAFT

IF YOU COULD OPEN YOUR OWN STORE, WHAT ITEMS WOULD YOU SELL? DESIGN THE EXTERIOR OF YOUR SHOP. THEN SHOW YOUR PRODUCTS IN THE DISPLAY WINDOW!

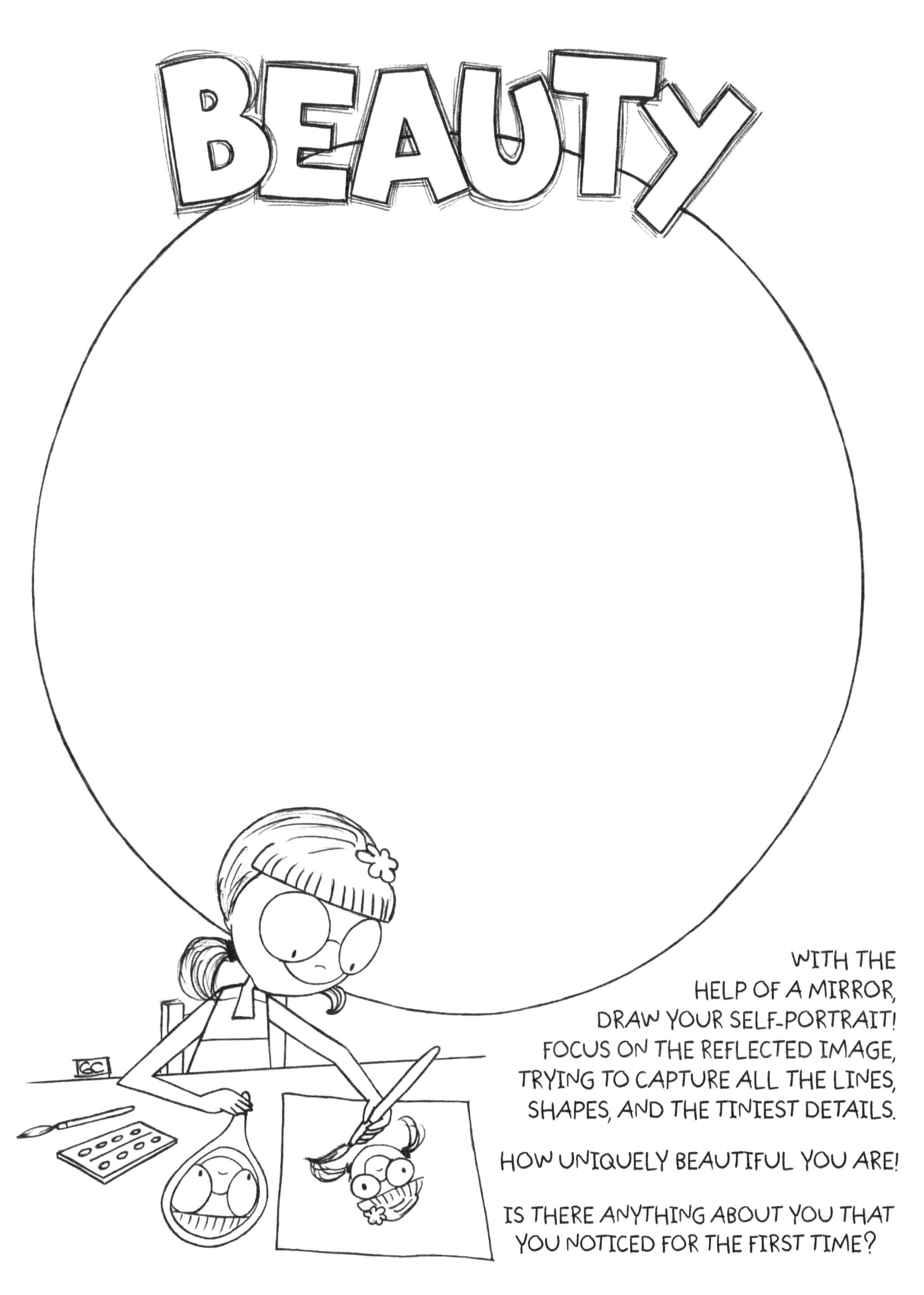

BEAUTY
WITH THE HELP OF A MIRROR, DRAW YOUR SELF-PORTRAIT! FOCUS ON THE REFLECTED IMAGE, TRYING TO CAPTURE ALL THE LINES, SHAPES, AND THE TINIEST DETAILS.
HOW UNIQUELY BEAUTIFUL YOU ARE!
IS THERE ANYTHING ABOUT YOU THAT YOU NOTICED FOR THE FIRST TIME?

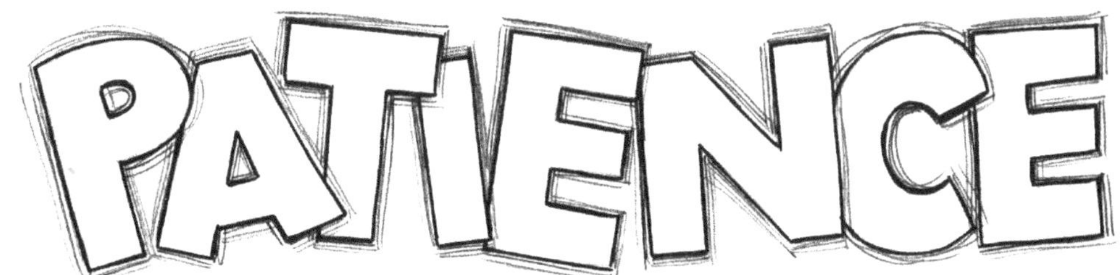

PATIENCE

THIS BLANK PAGE IS FOR YOU TO FILL IN WITH SKETCHES AND NOTES
WHILE YOU'RE PATIENTLY WAITING FOR SOMETHING TO HAPPEN.
IT WILL HELP YOU PASS THE TIME!

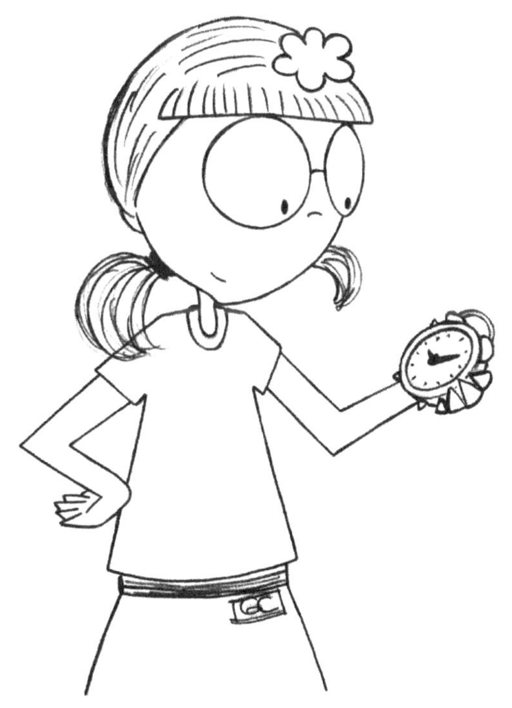

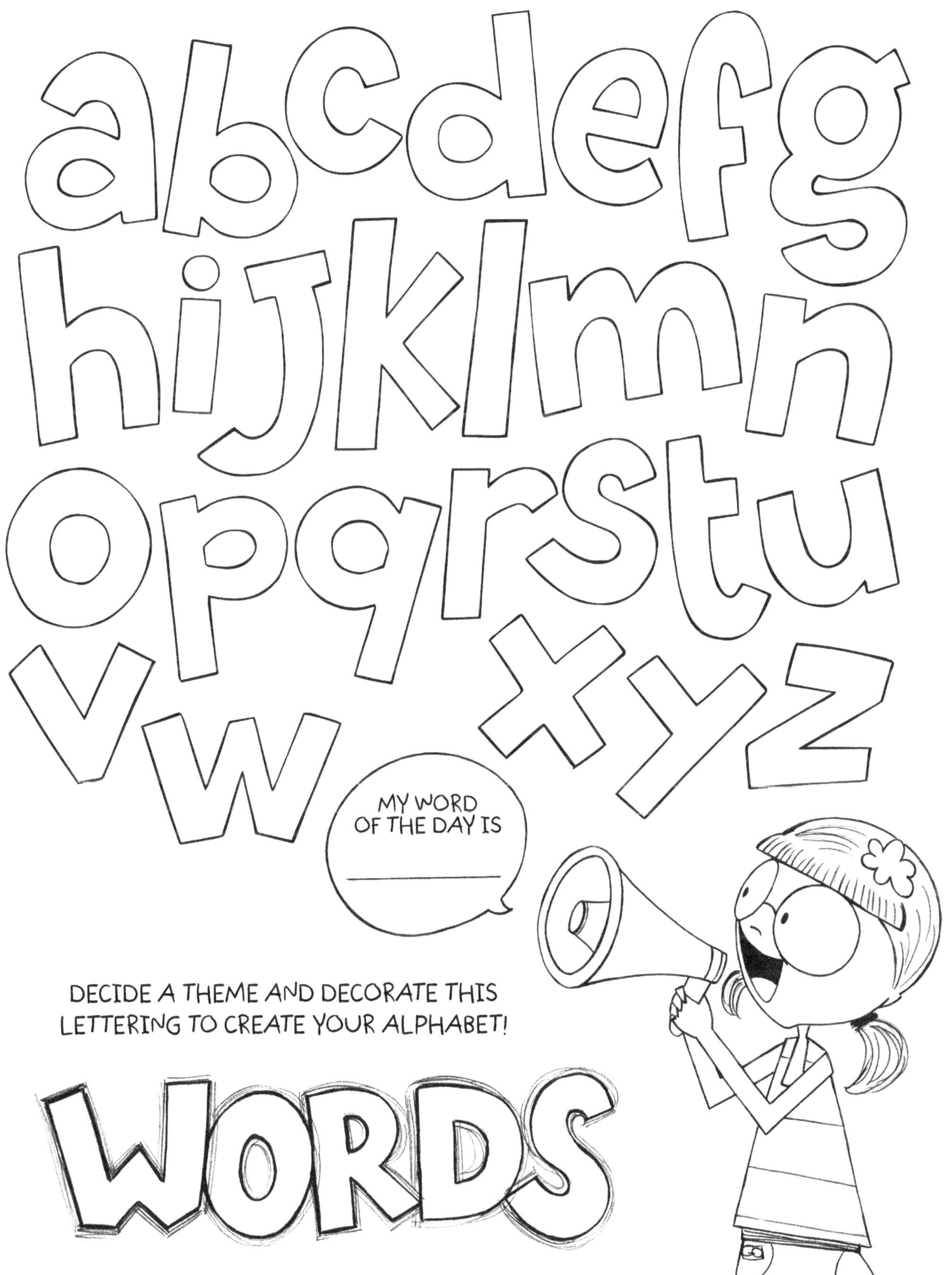

a b c d e f g
h i j k l m n
o p q r s t u
v w x y z
MY WORD OF THE DAY IS
DECIDE A THEME AND DECORATE THIS LETTERING TO CREATE YOUR ALPHABET!
WORDS

FLORA IS ALWAYS UP FOR TRAVELING!
THE EXCITING MOMENT SHE STARTS
PACKING HER SUITCASE,
AN AMAZING ADVENTURE BEGINS!

CHOOSE YOUR DESTINATION:

AND SKETCH THE ITEMS YOU
WOULD PUT INTO YOUR BAG!

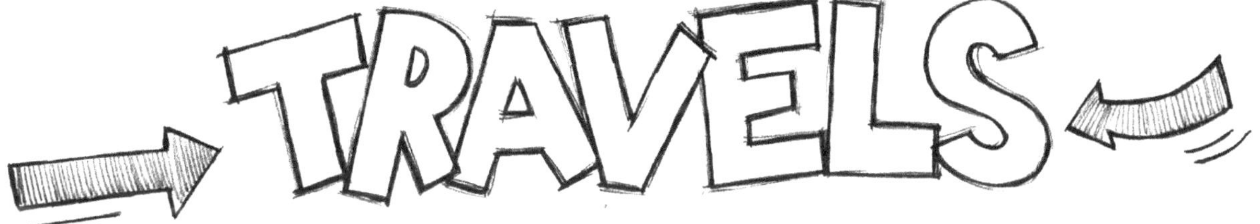

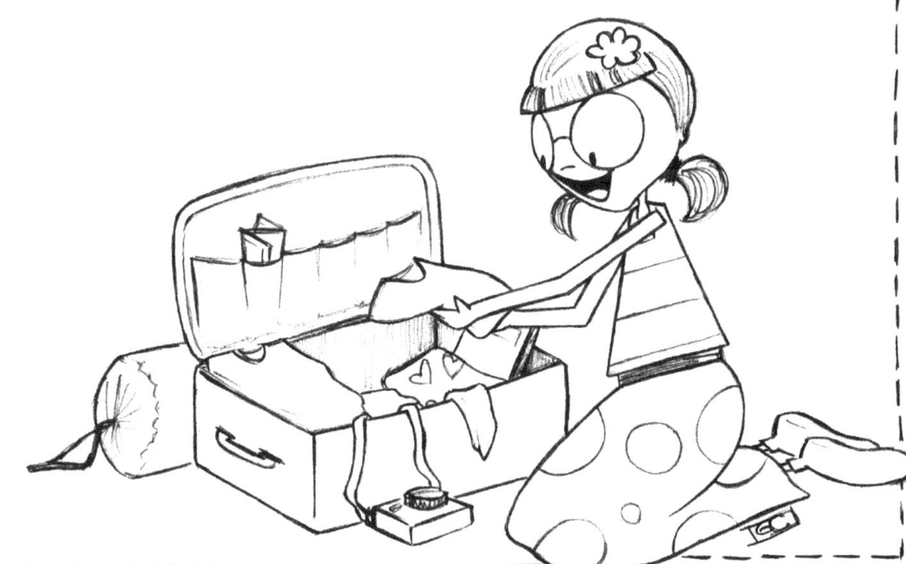

TRANSFORMATION

COMBINE SOME (OR ALL!) OF THESE ITEMS AND DRAW AN ECO-FRIENDLY SCENE OR AN ECO-HERO CHARACTER!
YOU MAY REUSE THE SAME OBJECTS AS MANY TIMES AS YOU WANT!!!

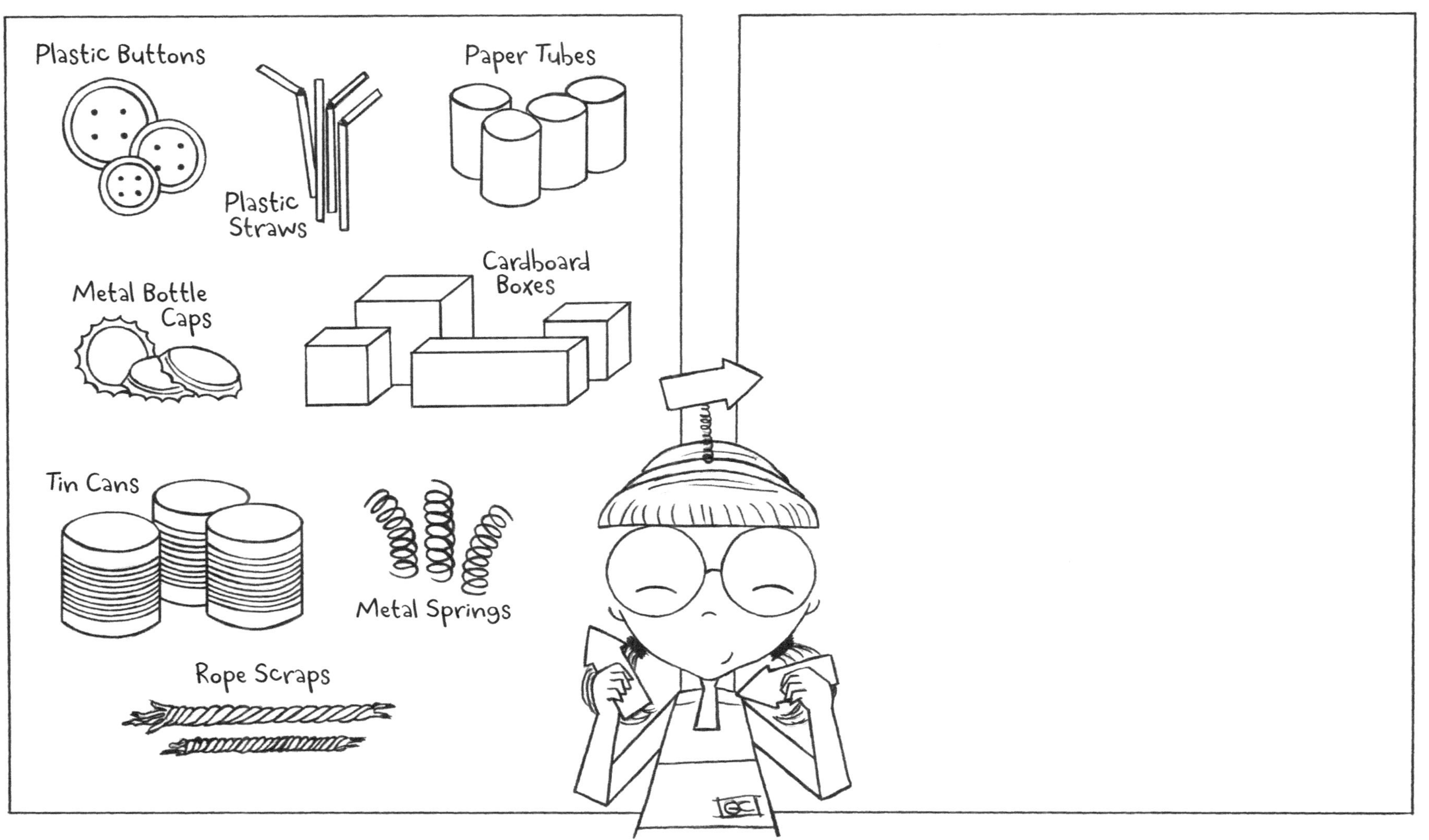

CHOOSE A PAIR OF OBJECTS, IDEAS, OR ADJECTIVES THAT ARE THE OPPOSITE OF EACH OTHER. THEN SKETCH EACH ONE IN SEPARATE SCENES. (FOR EXAMPLE NIGHT/DAY, ON/OFF, OLD/NEW...)

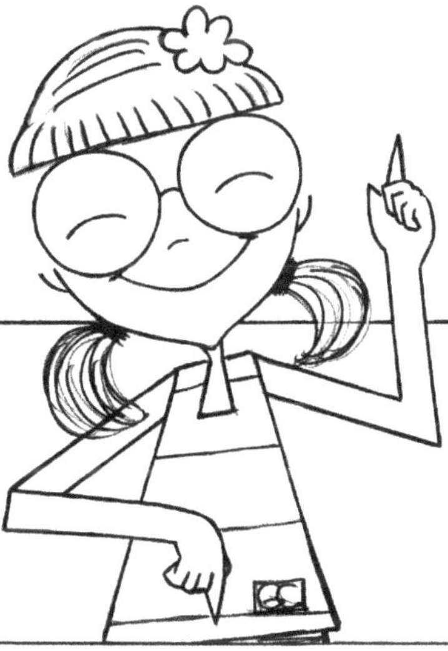

TECHNOLOGY

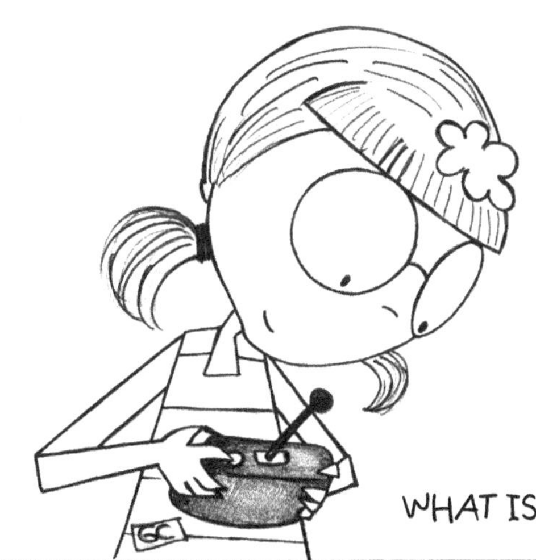

WHAT IS FLORA CONTROLLING?

STORIES

DESIGN TWO PUPPETS. THEN ADD SPEECH BALLOONS
OR THOUGHT BUBBLES TO CREATE A MINI STORY!

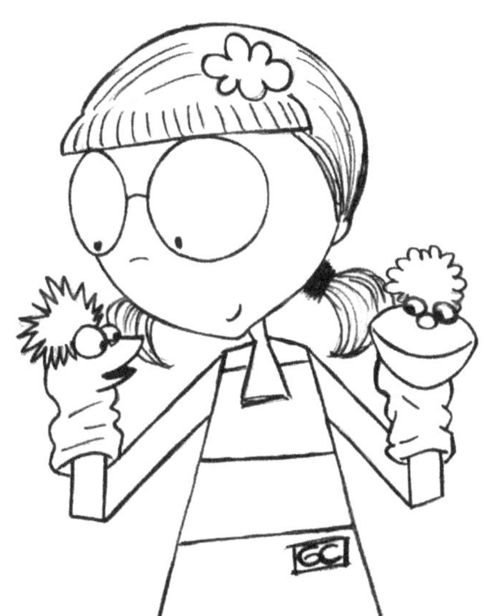

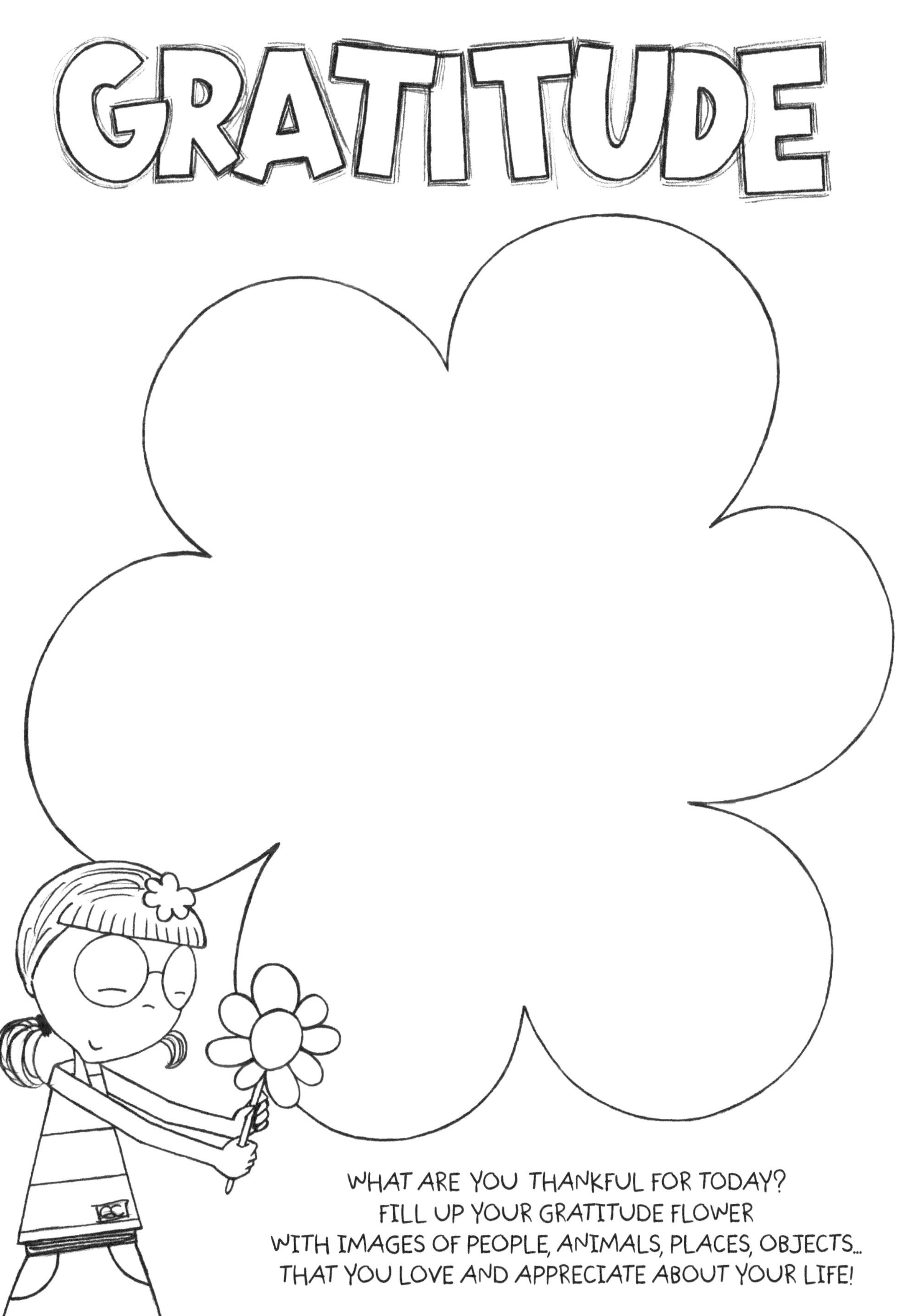

GRATITUDE
WHAT ARE YOU THANKFUL FOR TODAY?
FILL UP YOUR GRATITUDE FLOWER
WITH IMAGES OF PEOPLE, ANIMALS, PLACES, OBJECTS...
THAT YOU LOVE AND APPRECIATE ABOUT YOUR LIFE!

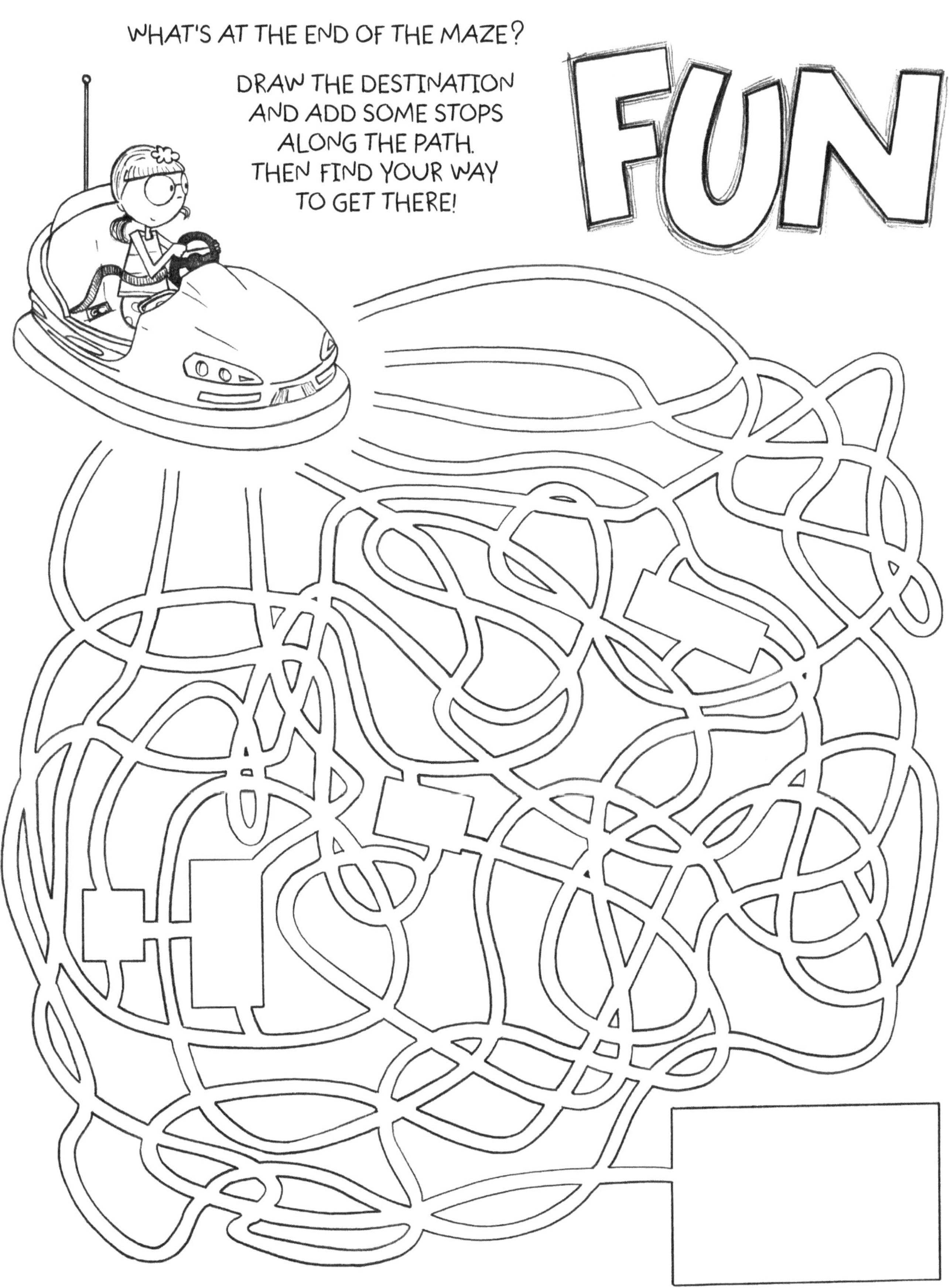

WHAT'S AT THE END OF THE MAZE?
DRAW THE DESTINATION AND ADD SOME STOPS ALONG THE PATH. THEN FIND YOUR WAY TO GET THERE!
FUN

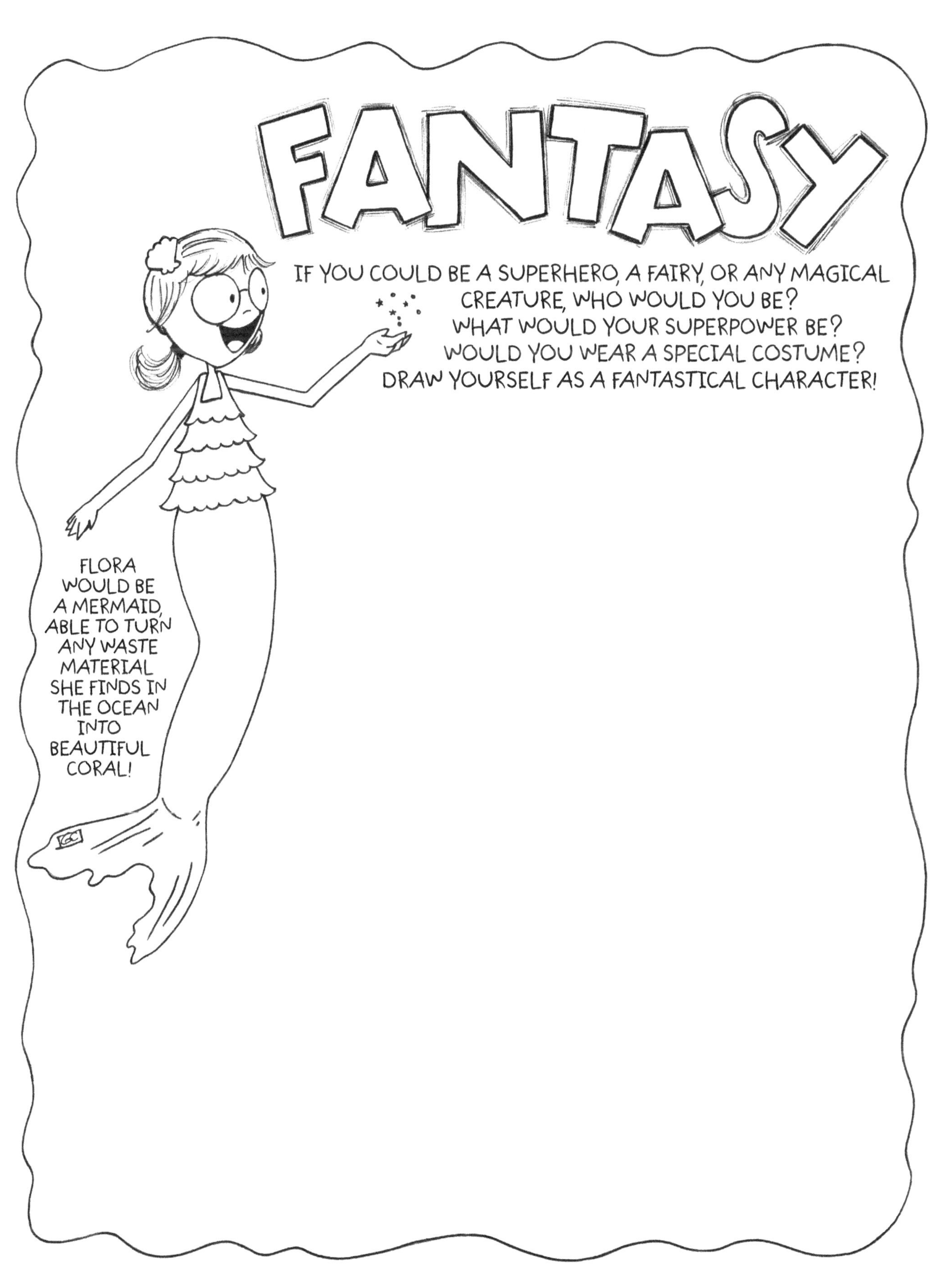

FANTASY

IF YOU COULD BE A SUPERHERO, A FAIRY, OR ANY MAGICAL
CREATURE, WHO WOULD YOU BE?
WHAT WOULD YOUR SUPERPOWER BE?
WOULD YOU WEAR A SPECIAL COSTUME?
DRAW YOURSELF AS A FANTASTICAL CHARACTER!

FLORA WOULD BE A MERMAID, ABLE TO TURN ANY WASTE MATERIAL SHE FINDS IN THE OCEAN INTO BEAUTIFUL CORAL!

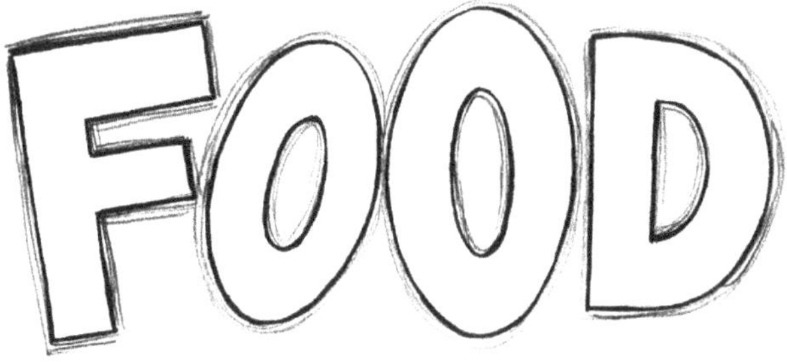

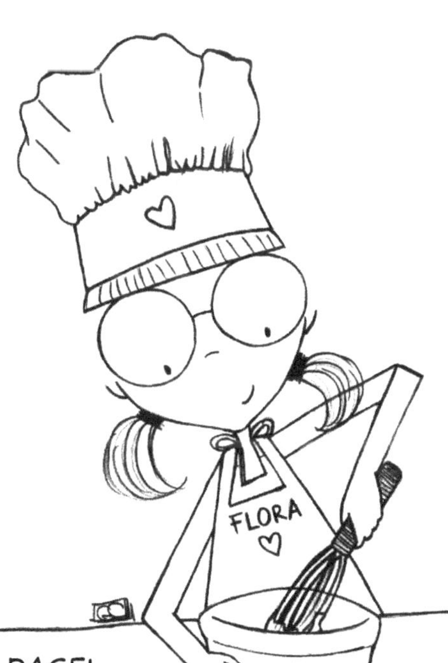

DESIGN A COOKBOOK PAGE!
TODAY'S SPECIAL IS: _______________

DRAW THE INGREDIENTS
OF YOUR FAVORITE DISH OR
CREATE YOUR OWN SECRET RECIPE!

FAMILY

HOW MANY MEMBERS ARE THERE IN YOUR FAMILY? WHAT ARE THEIR NAMES AND SOME OF THEIR QUALITIES? IF YOU HAD TO REPRESENT THEM USING OBJECTS, WHAT WOULD YOU CHOOSE? DRAW THREE THINGS FOR EACH FAMILY MEMBER THAT REMIND YOU OF THEM!

GENEROSITY

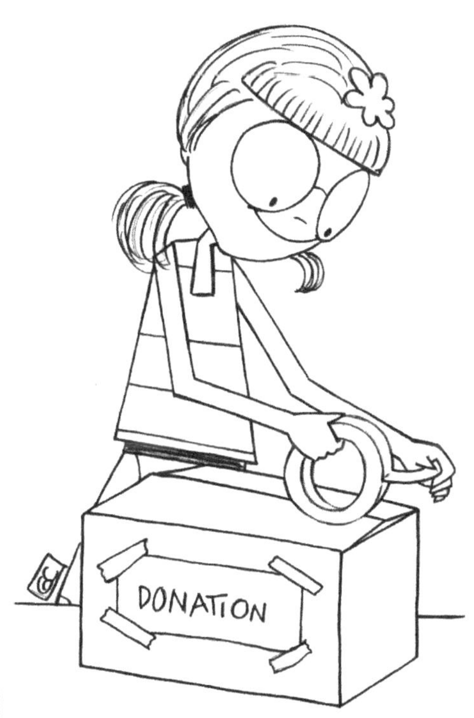

WHAT'S SOMETHING YOU CAN DO
TO HELP OTHERS TODAY?

EXPLORATION

WHAT ENVIRONMENT IS FLORA EXPLORING? DESIGN A BACKGROUND AND CREATE A SCENE ALL AROUND HER!

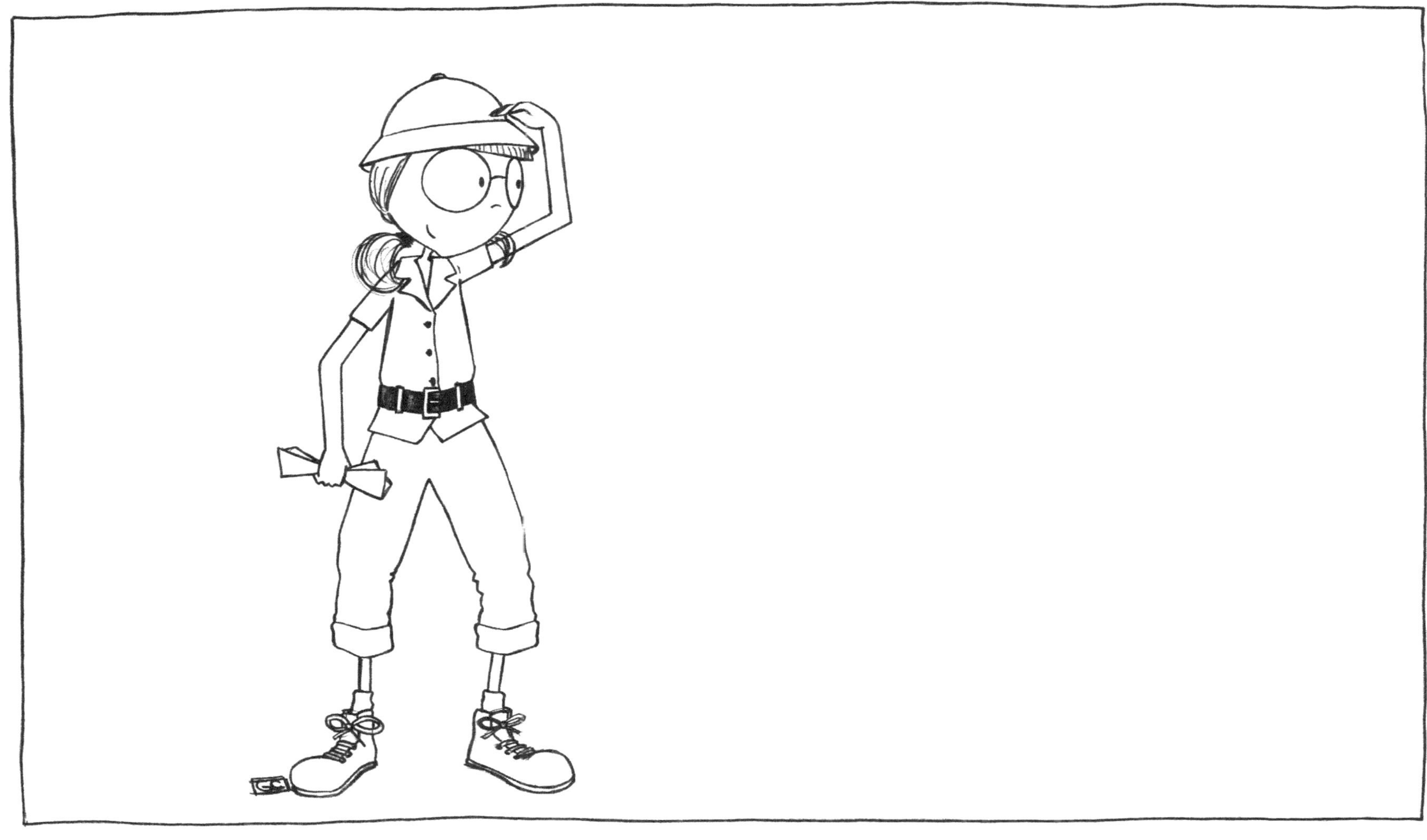

ENERGY

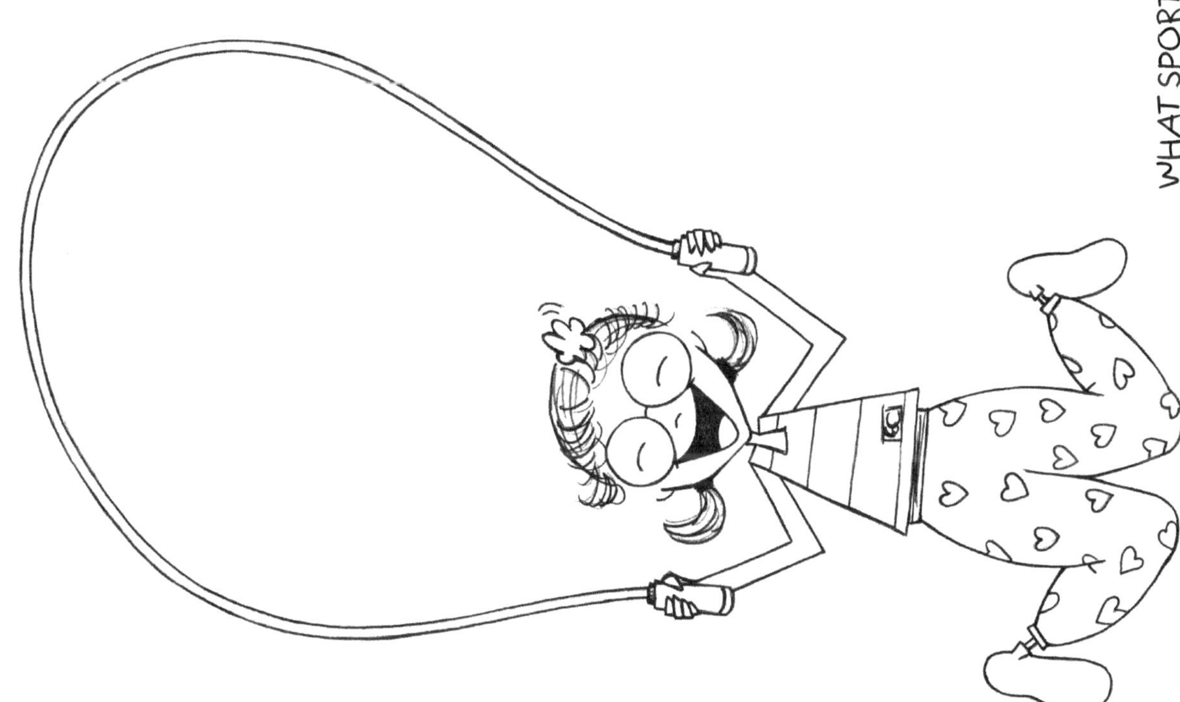

WHAT SPORT OR PHYSICAL ACTIVITY DO YOU LIKE TO DO FOR EXERCISE?

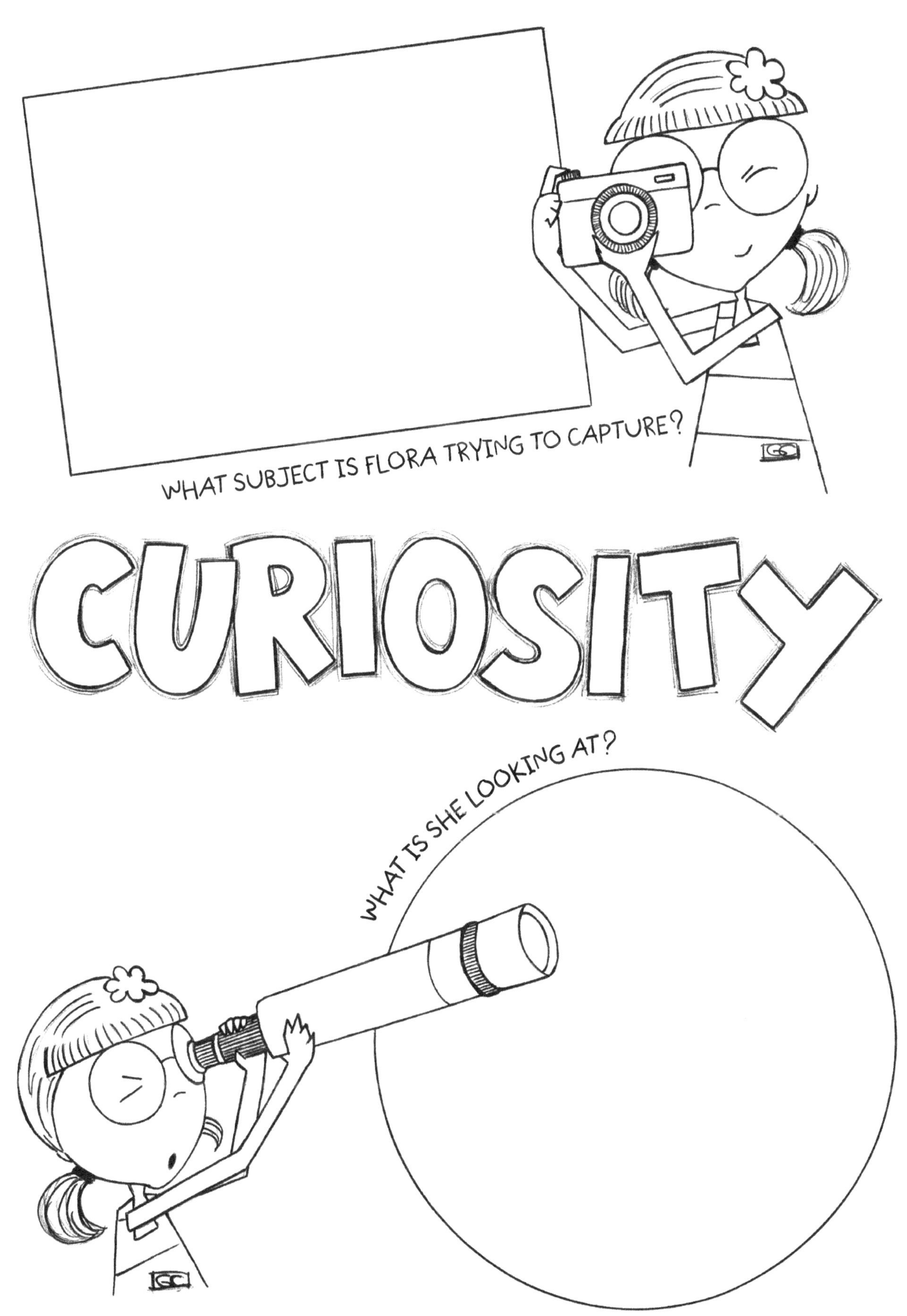

WHAT SUBJECT IS FLORA TRYING TO CAPTURE?
CURIOSITY
WHAT IS SHE LOOKING AT?

DREAMS

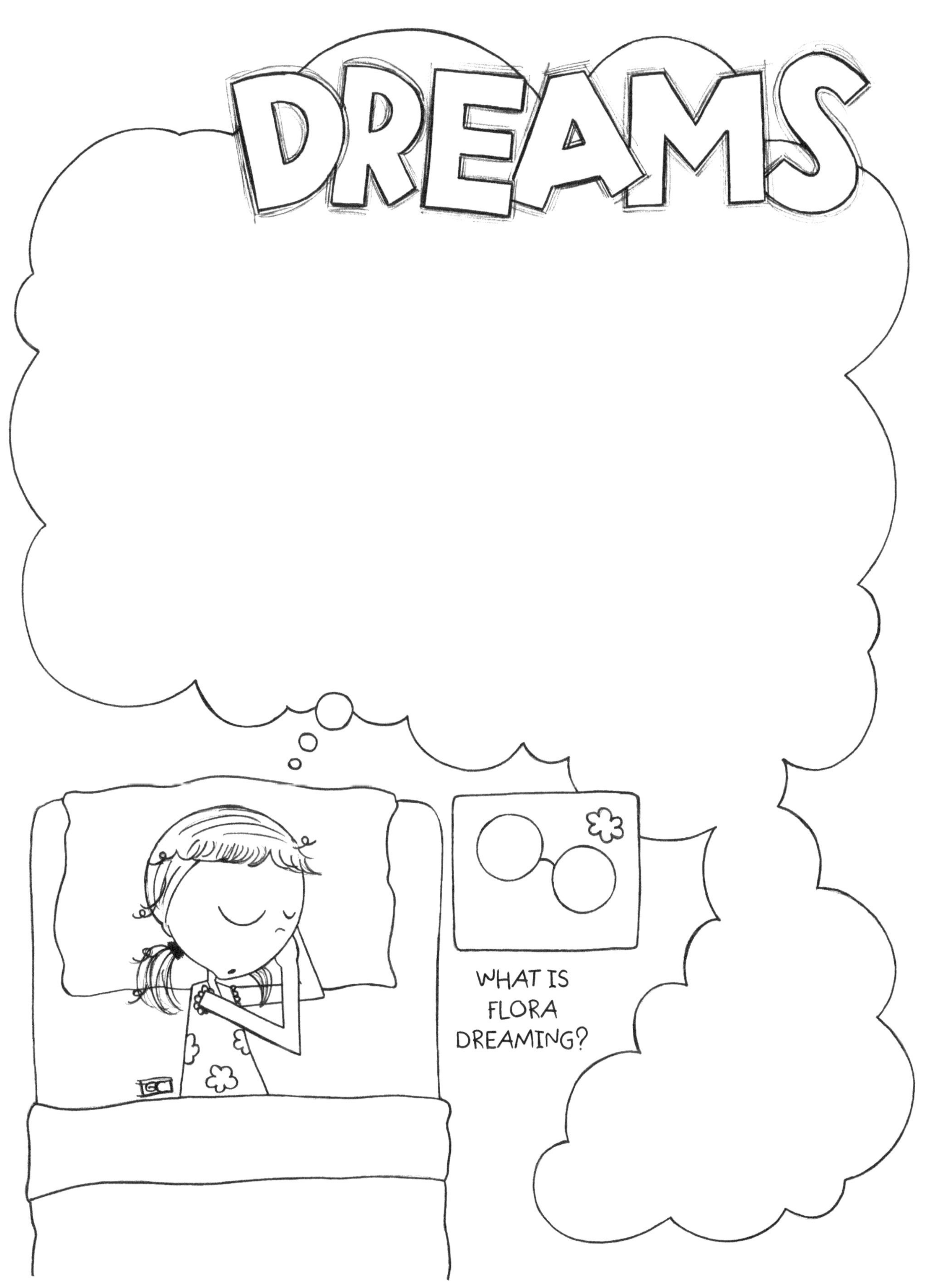

CELEBRATION

THINK ABOUT YOUR QUALITIES, ABILITIES, SKILLS, OR SOME OF THE ACCOMPLISHMENTS YOU ARE MOST PROUD OF, AND CREATE THE AWARD YOU DESERVE! DECORATE YOUR MEDAL WITH IMAGES AND WORDS TO CELEBRATE YOUR UNIQUENESS!

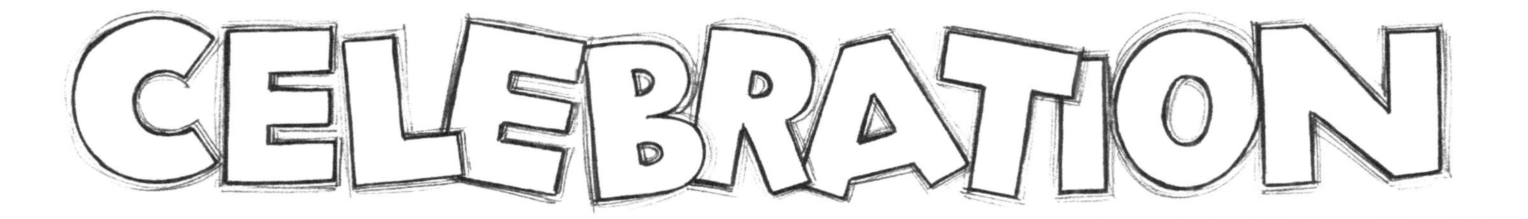

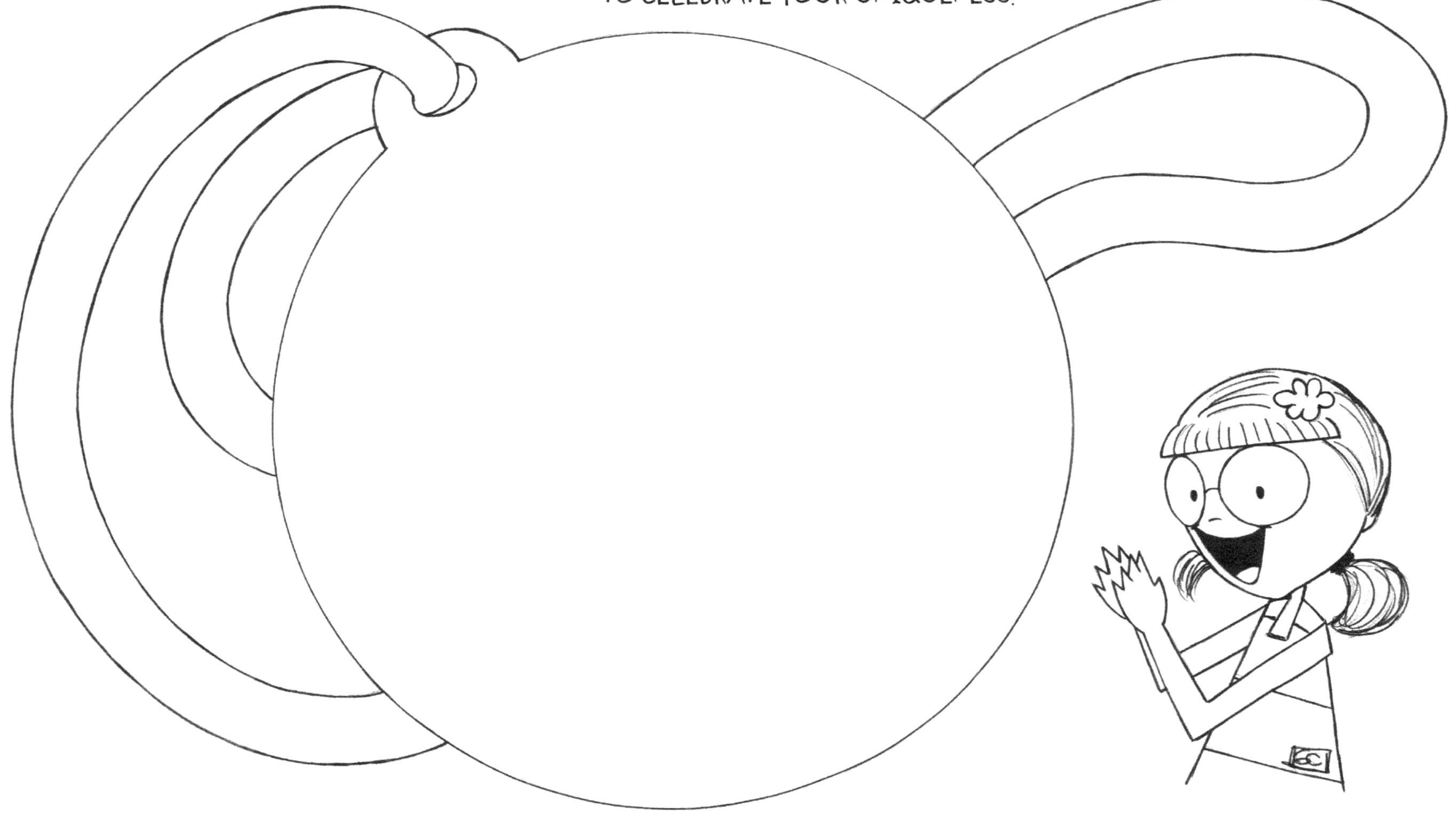

CHOOSE A MASTERPIECE FROM ART HISTORY
AND RECREATE IT IN YOUR OWN STYLE!

TITLE:_______________________________

ARTIST:_______________________________

ART

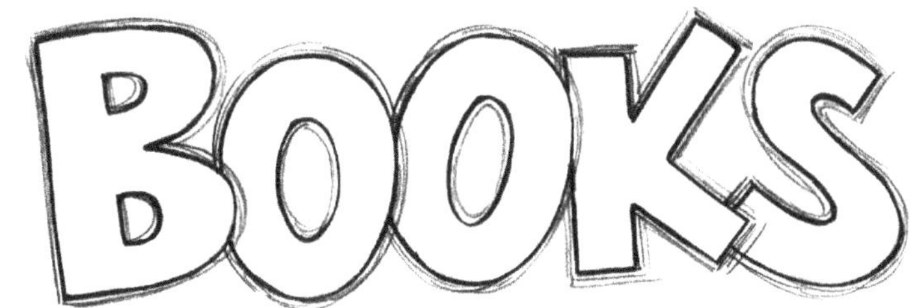

BOOKS

ILLUSTRATE A SCENE FROM YOUR FAVORITE BOOK!

BOOK TITLE: _______________________________

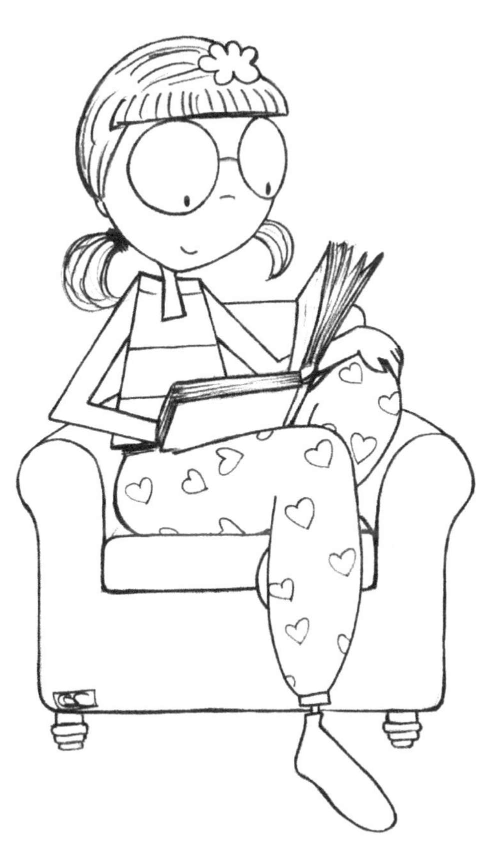

CREATIVITY

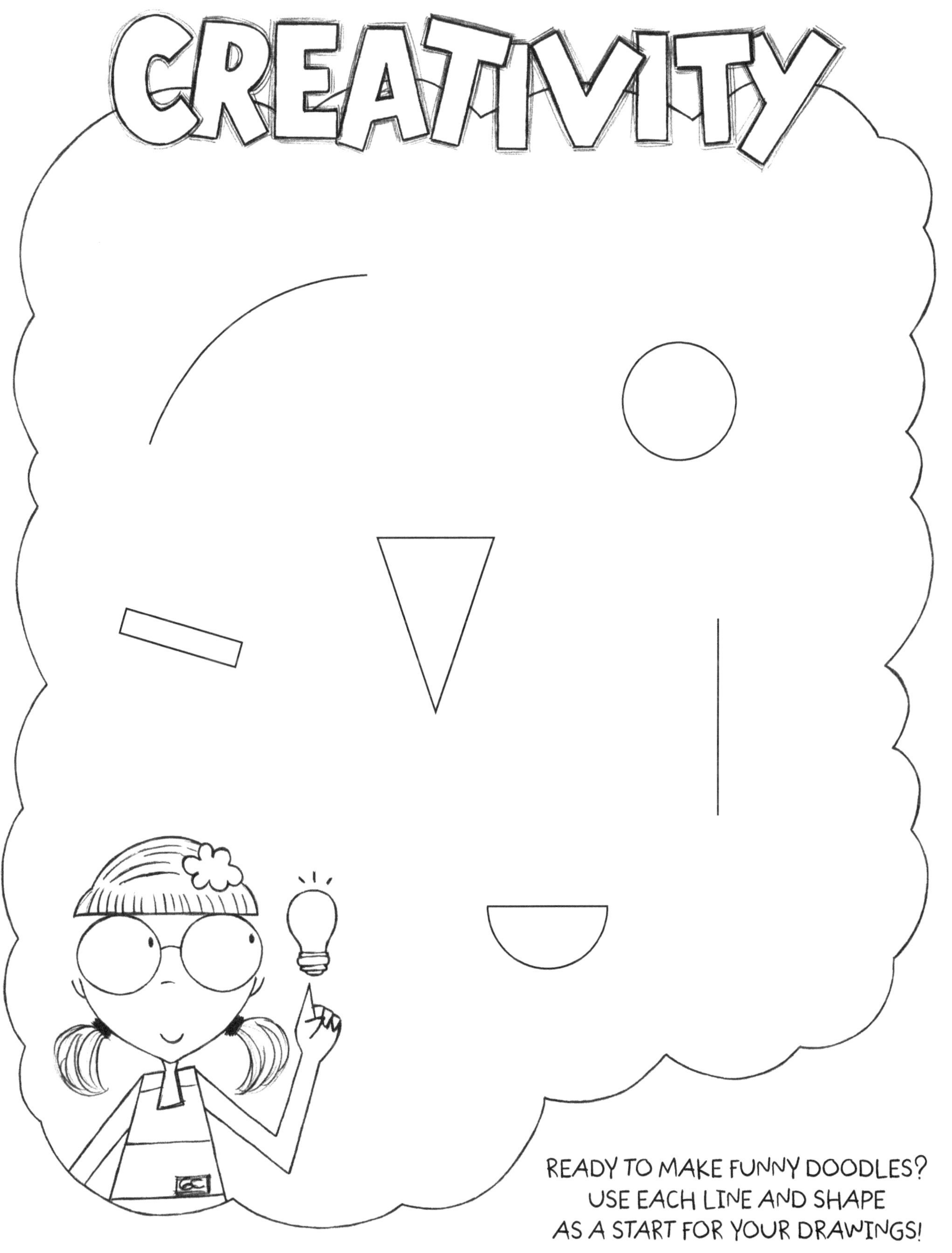

READY TO MAKE FUNNY DOODLES?
USE EACH LINE AND SHAPE
AS A START FOR YOUR DRAWINGS!

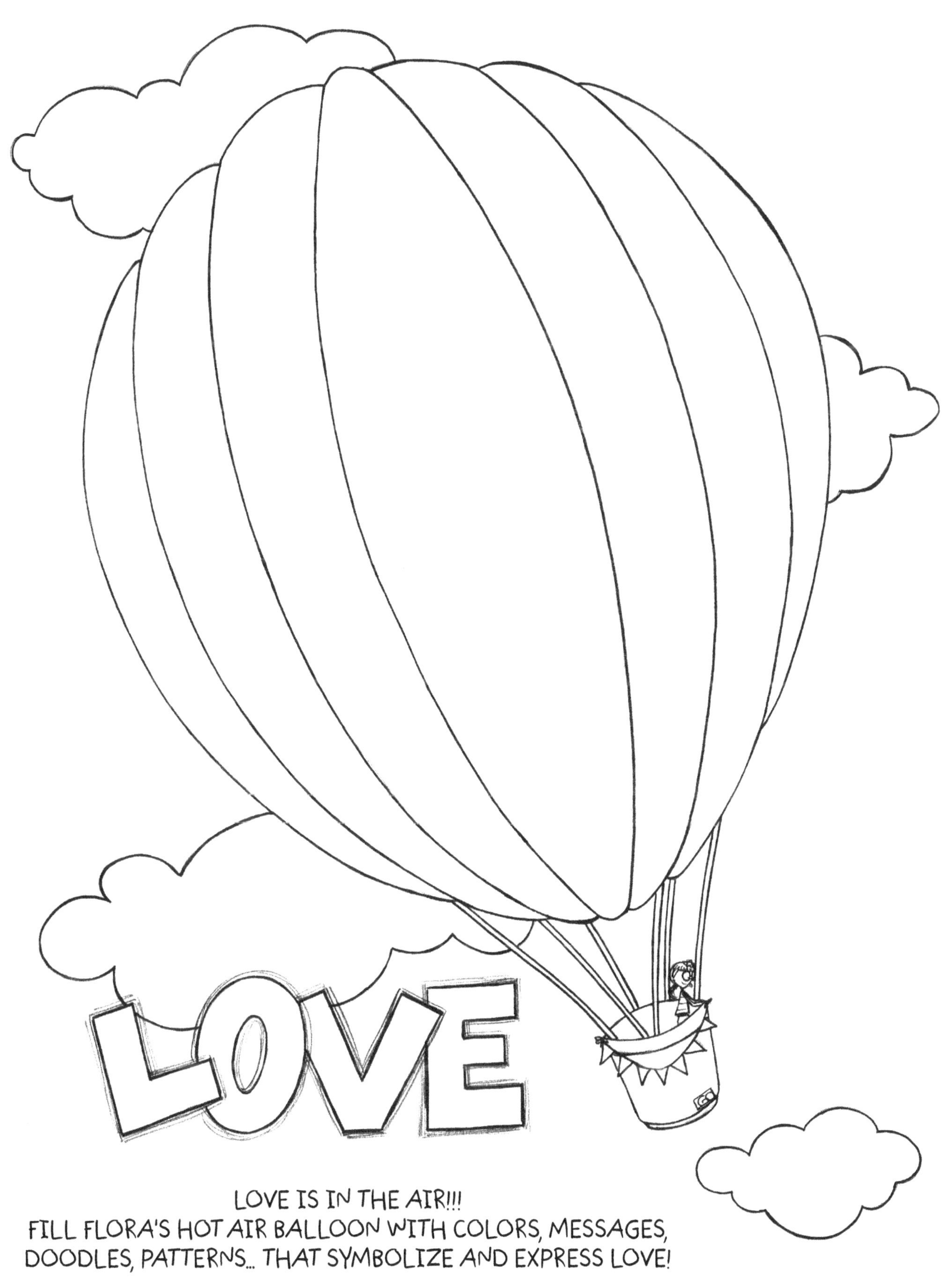

LOVE IS IN THE AIR!!!
FILL FLORA'S HOT AIR BALLOON WITH COLORS, MESSAGES,
DOODLES, PATTERNS... THAT SYMBOLIZE AND EXPRESS LOVE!

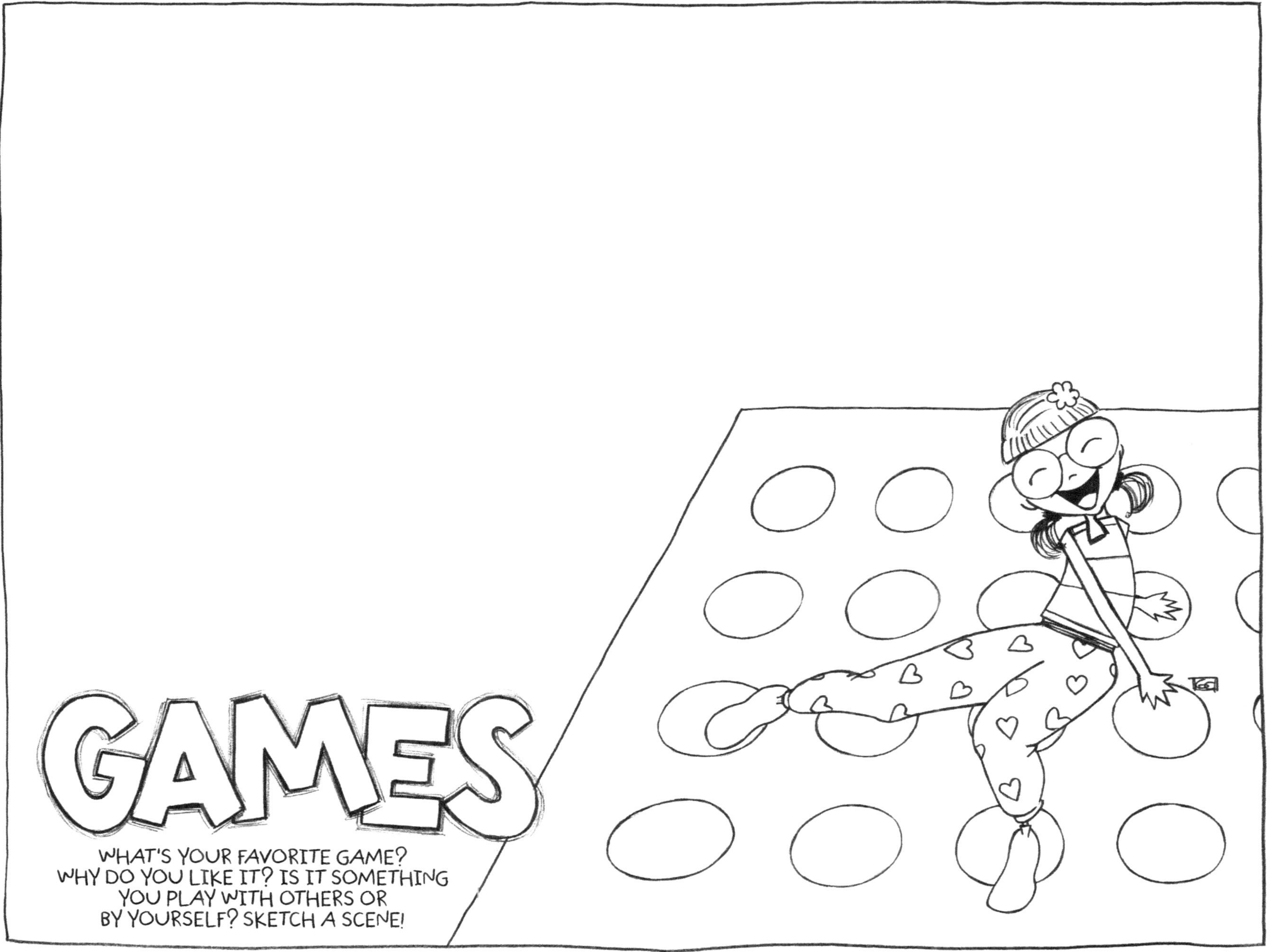

GAMES
WHAT'S YOUR FAVORITE GAME?
WHY DO YOU LIKE IT? IS IT SOMETHING
YOU PLAY WITH OTHERS OR
BY YOURSELF? SKETCH A SCENE!

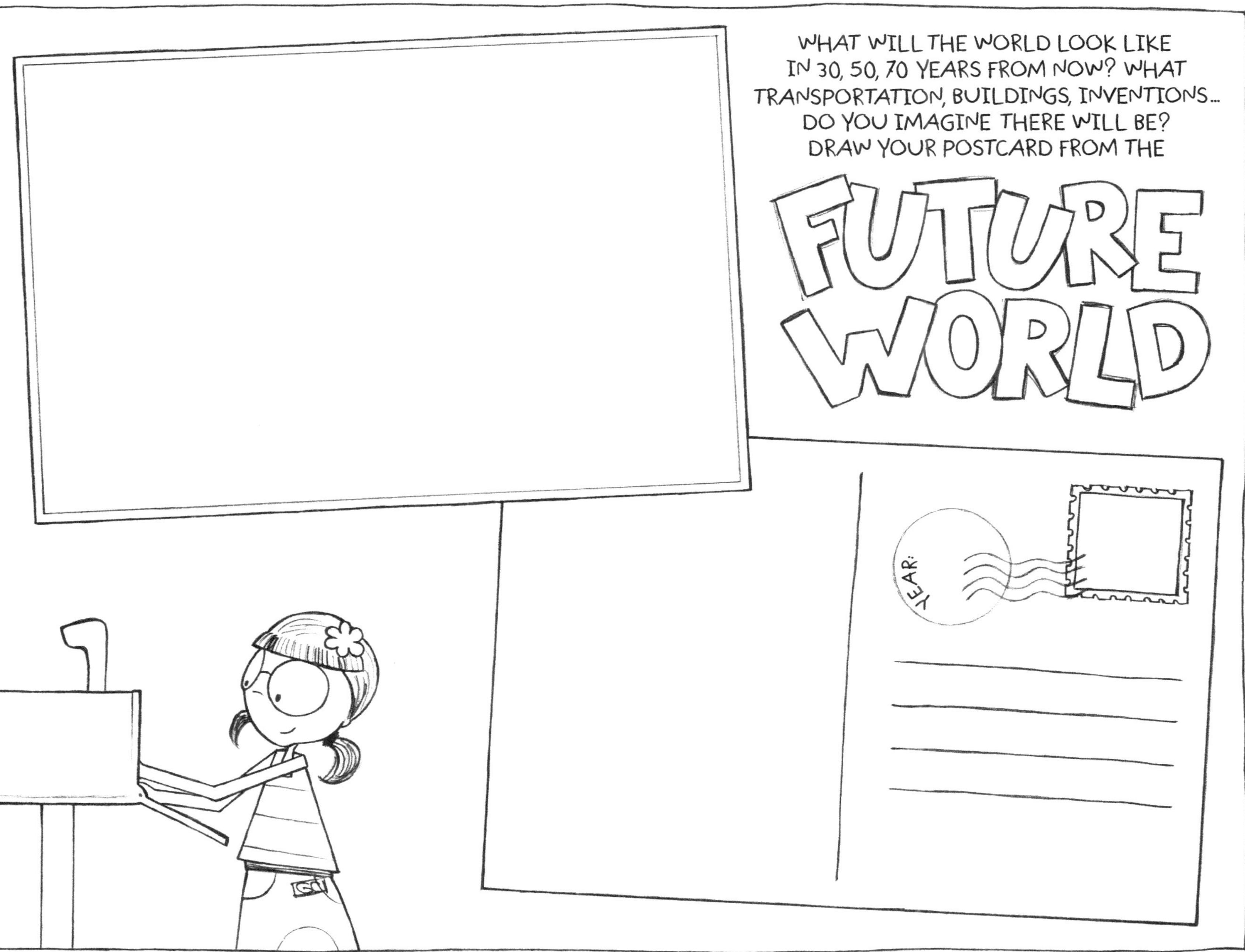

WHAT WILL THE WORLD LOOK LIKE IN 30, 50, 70 YEARS FROM NOW? WHAT TRANSPORTATION, BUILDINGS, INVENTIONS... DO YOU IMAGINE THERE WILL BE? DRAW YOUR POSTCARD FROM THE
FUTURE WORLD
YEAR:

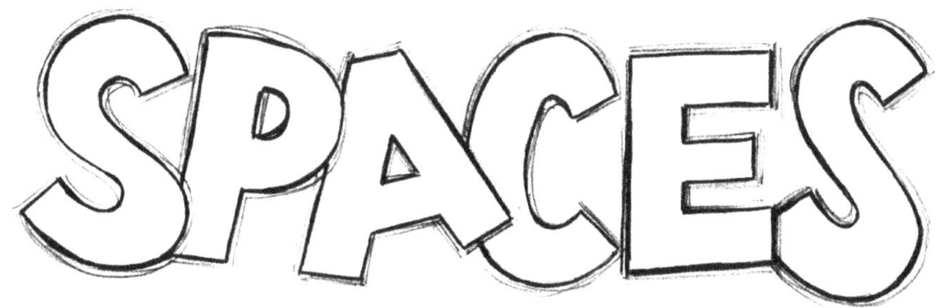

WHAT'S ON THE OTHER SIDE OF THE WINDOW?
IS FLORA INSIDE LOOKING OUT OR OUTSIDE LOOKING IN???
SKETCH YOUR VIEW!

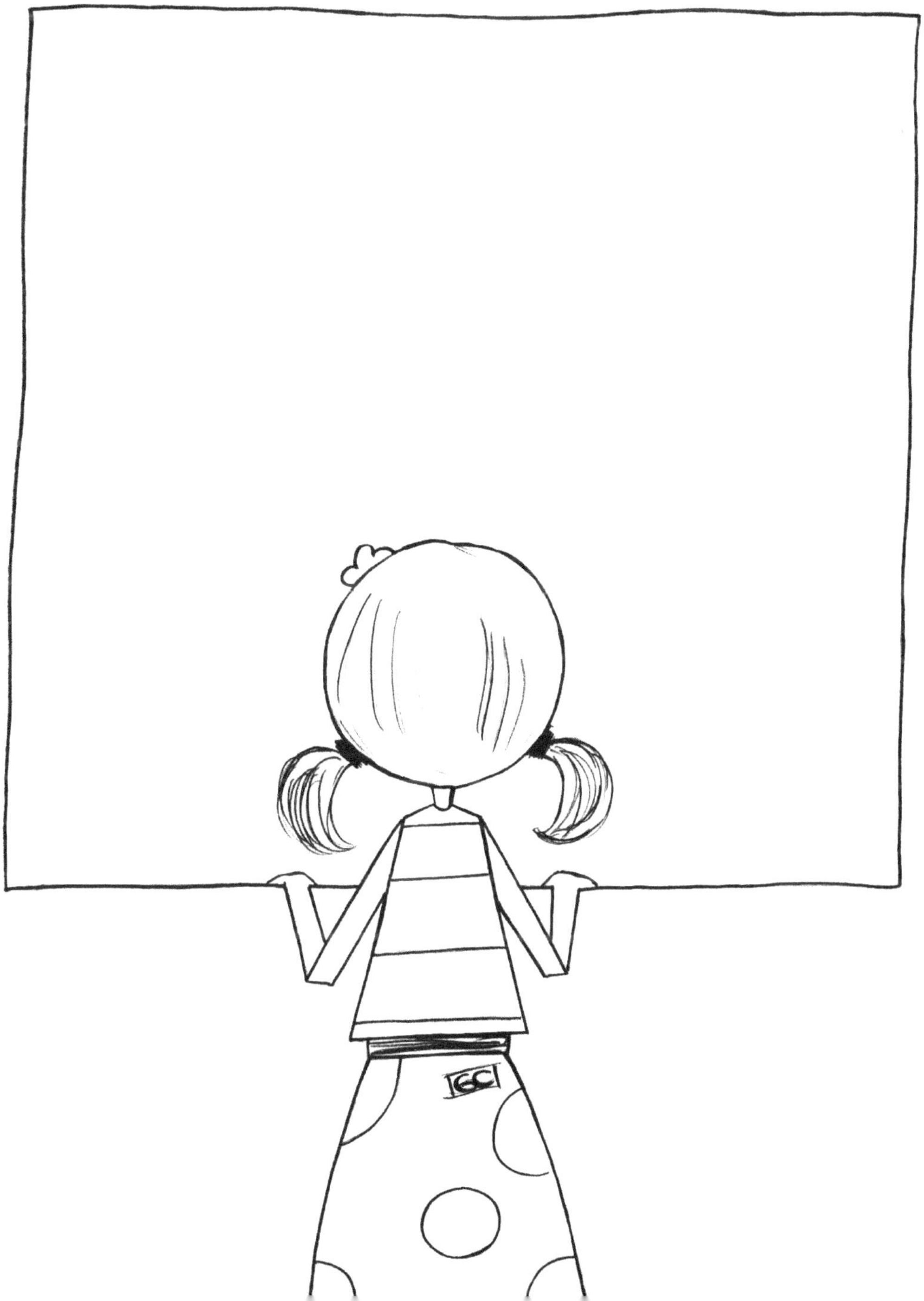

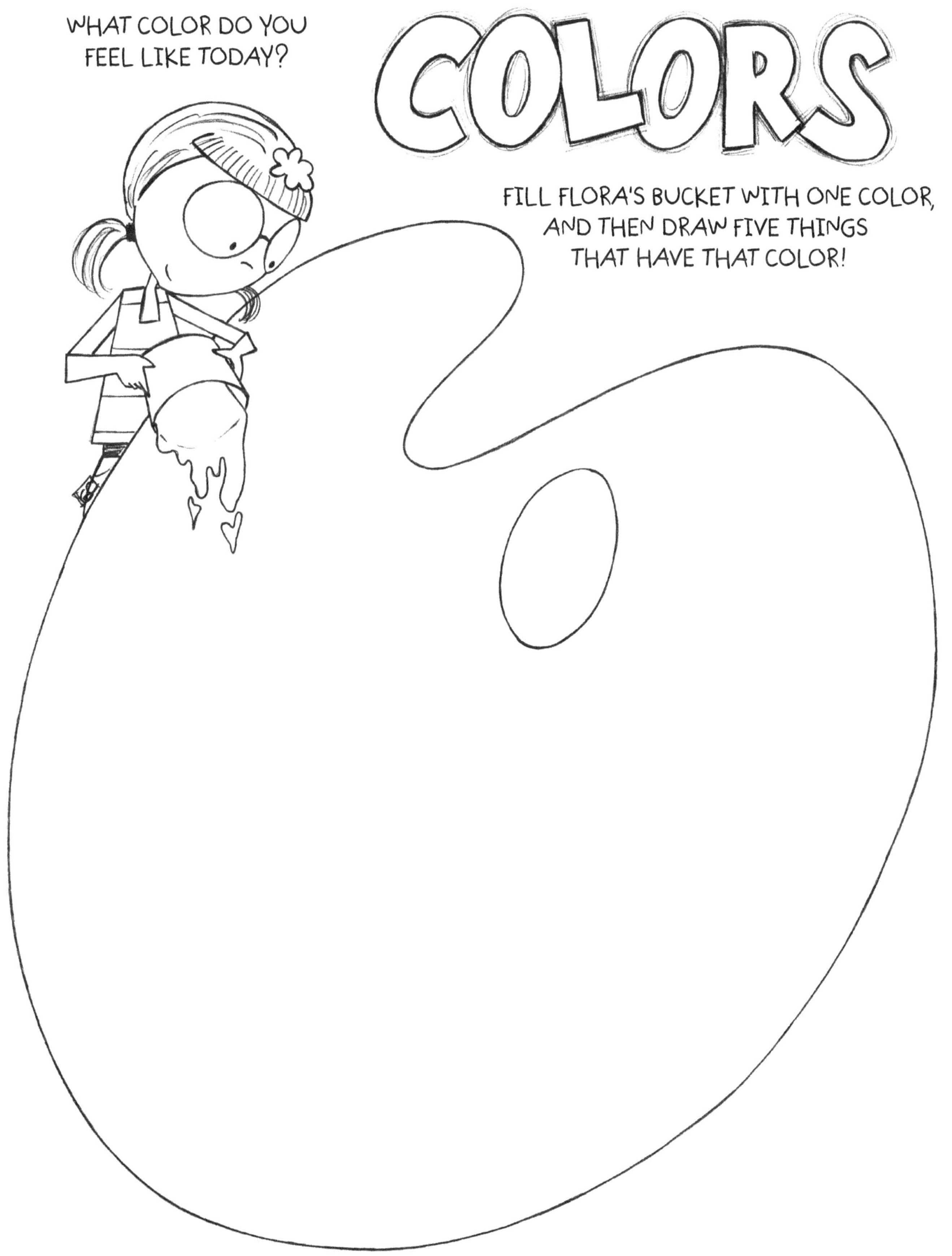

WHAT COLOR DO YOU
FEEL LIKE TODAY?

COLORS

FILL FLORA'S BUCKET WITH ONE COLOR,
AND THEN DRAW FIVE THINGS
THAT HAVE THAT COLOR!

ANIMALS

WHAT ANIMAL BEST REPRESENTS YOU? WHY?

IF YOU WERE AN ANIMAL, YOU WOULD BE ___________

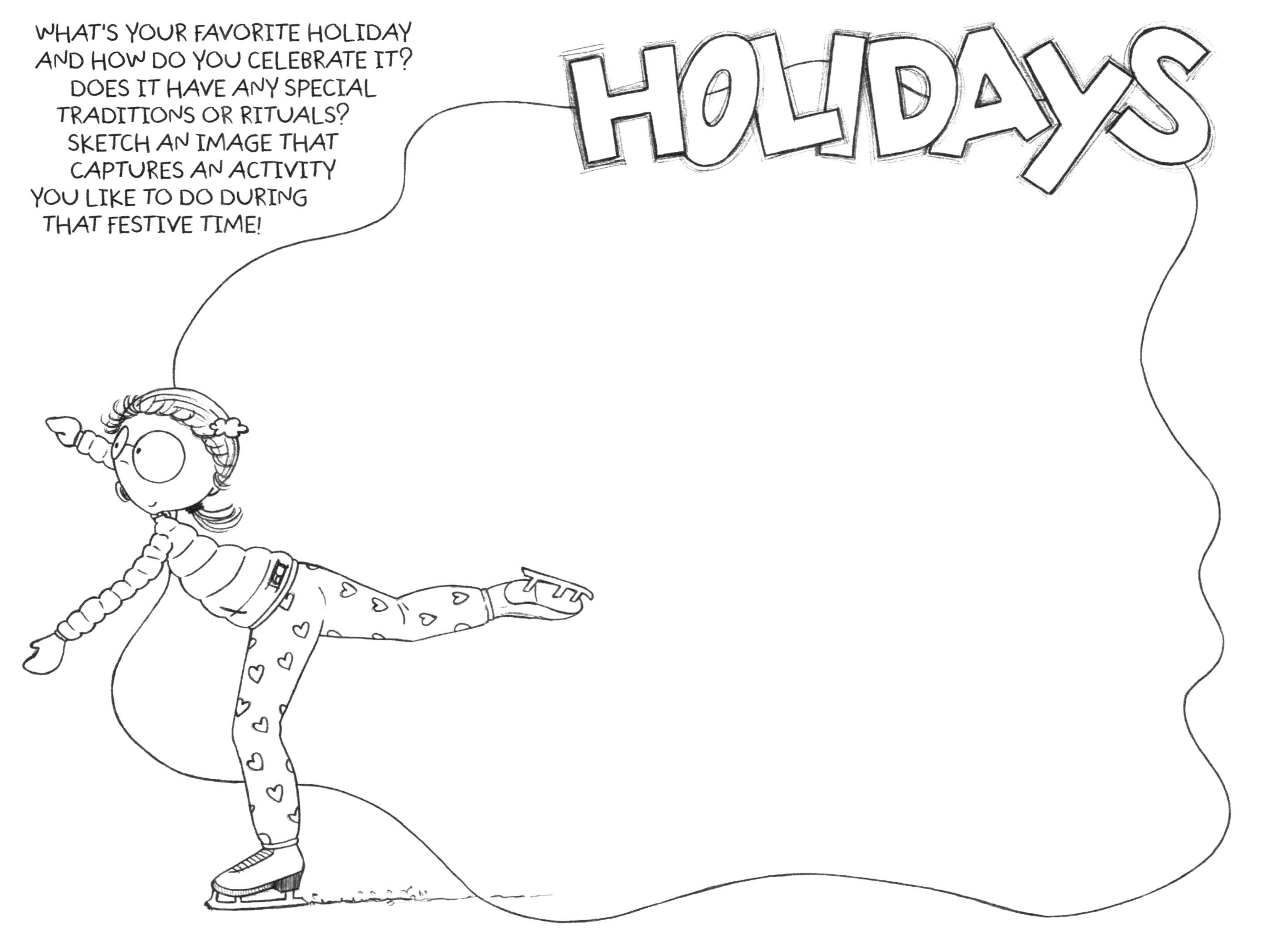

HOLIDAYS
WHAT'S YOUR FAVORITE HOLIDAY AND HOW DO YOU CELEBRATE IT? DOES IT HAVE ANY SPECIAL TRADITIONS OR RITUALS? SKETCH AN IMAGE THAT CAPTURES AN ACTIVITY YOU LIKE TO DO DURING THAT FESTIVE TIME!

HAPPINESS

CREATE YOUR HAPPINESS MOOD BOARD! FILL UP THE PAGE WITH IMAGES, COLORS, WORDS... THAT MAKE YOU FEEL HAPPY!

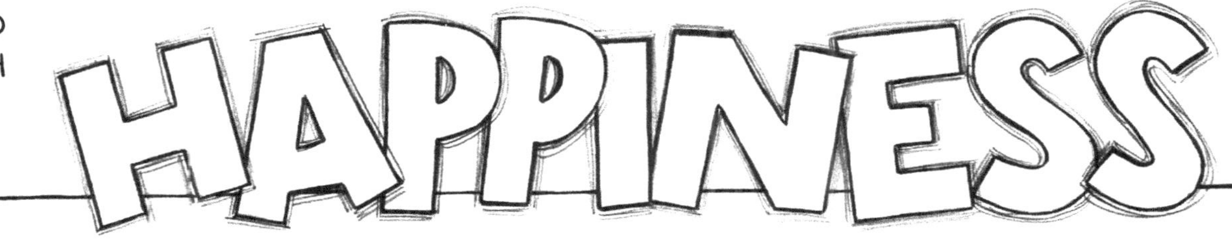
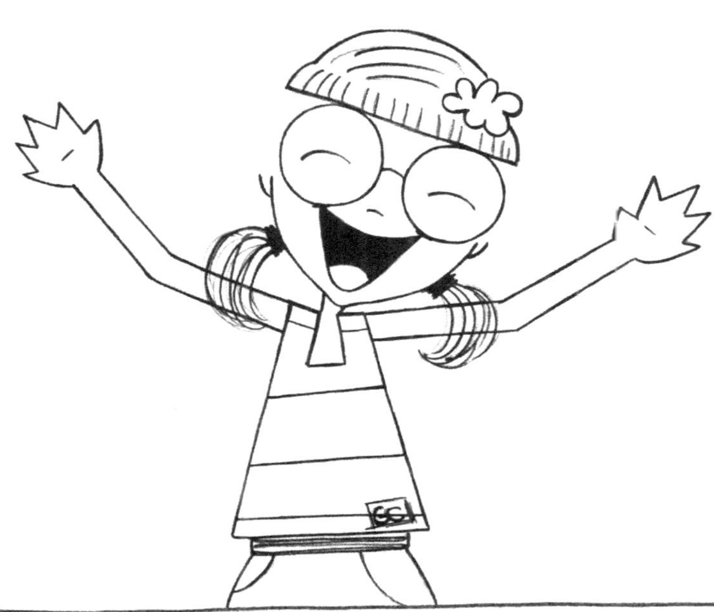

REMINDERS

FLORA IS SENDING YOU IMPORTANT MESSAGES TODAY!!!
ADD YOUR OWN REMINDER. THEN COLOR AND CUT THEM ALL OUT!
PUT THEM IN A PLACE WHERE YOU CAN EASILY SEE THEM WHENEVER YOU NEED TO!

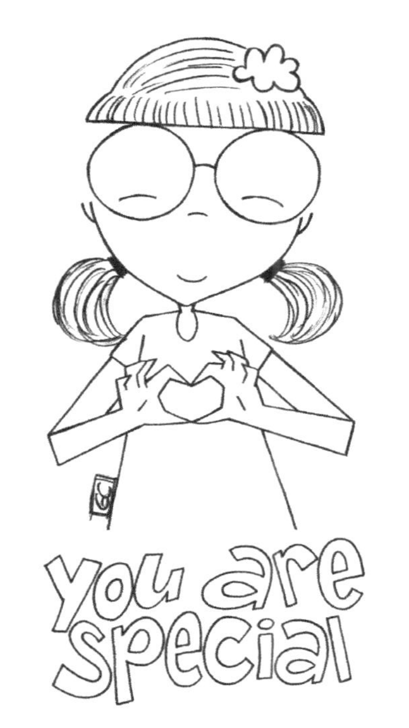

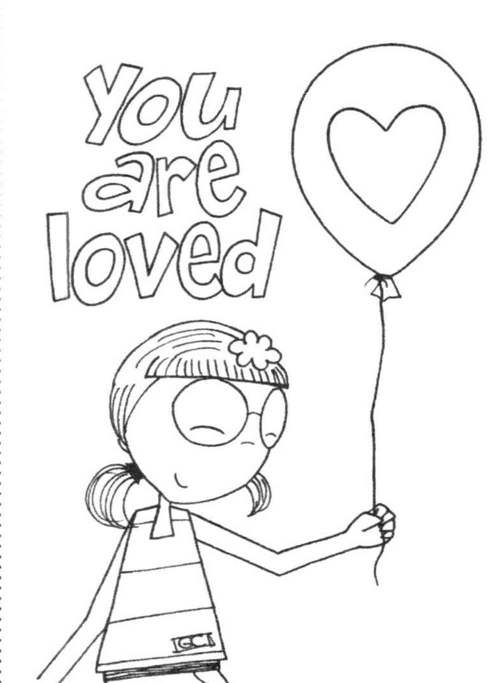

Dear Friend, I hope you had fun creating with Flora!

THANK YOU!!!!!
I can't wait to hear from you!

Send your thoughts, comments, and feedback to flora@floramakesmesmile.com!

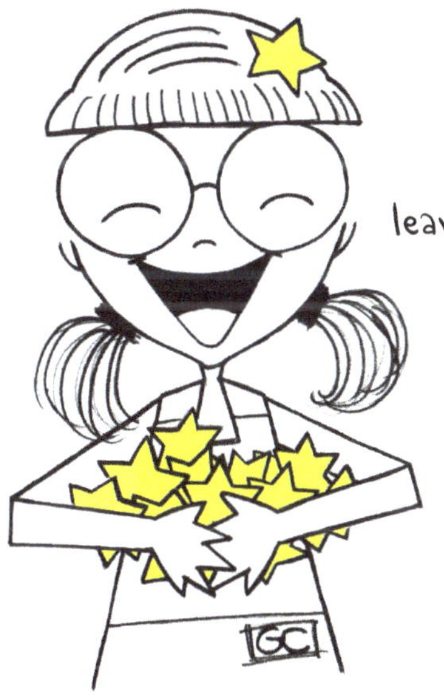

If you enjoyed the book, please consider leaving a review wherever you bought it from!

Your help in spreading the word does make a difference!

Share your works of art on social media using the hashtag #floramakesmesmile! I would love to see what you've created!!!

(to all friends under 18 years old, ask your grown-up for permission before posting your photos!)

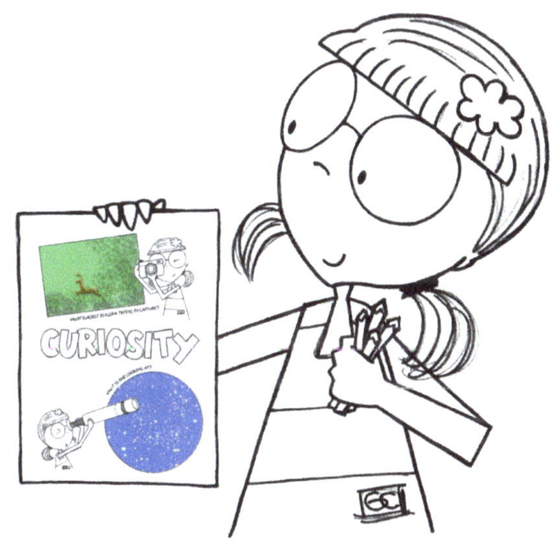

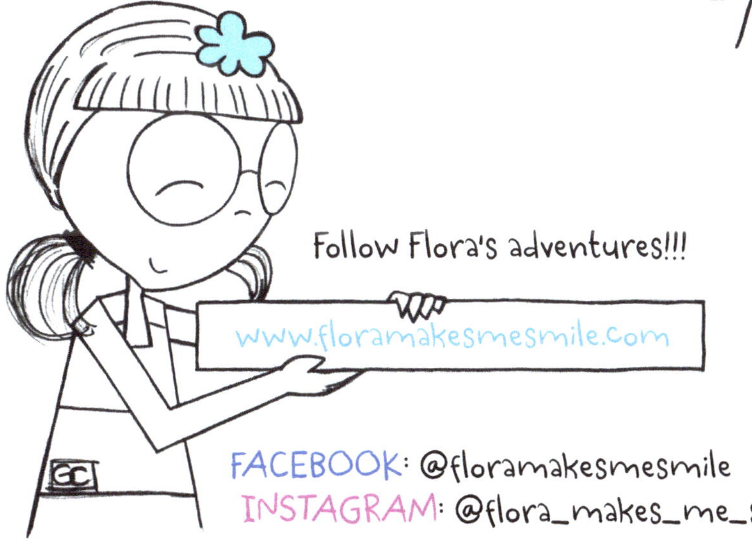

Follow Flora's adventures!!!

www.floramakesmesmile.com

FACEBOOK: @floramakesmesmile
INSTAGRAM: @flora_makes_me_smile